(Issued with Army Orders Dated 1st June 1918.)

REGULATIONS FOR THE

QUEEN MARY'S ARMY AUXILIARY CORPS

1918

The Naval & Military Press Ltd

Published by
The Naval & Military Press Ltd
5 Riverside, Brambleside, Bellbrook
Industrial Estate, Uckfield, East Sussex,
TN22 1QQ England

Tel: +44 (0) 1825 749494
Fax: +44 (0) 1825 765701
www.naval-military-press.com
www.military-genealogy.com
www.militarymaproom.com

In reprinting in facsimile from the original, any imperfections are inevitably reproduced and the quality may fall short of modern type and cartographic standards.

REGULATIONS FOR THE QUEEN MARY'S ARMY AUXILIARY CORPS.

CONTENTS.

Paragraph.	—

1	Definitions.
	Organization.
	    A. Mobile Branch.
	    B. Immobile Branch.

2	Object.
	    A. General Substitution.
	    B. Motor Drivers Overseas.
	    C. Proportionate Substitution.
	    D. Substitution at Home.
	    E. Conditions of Substitution.
	    F. Substitution in Convalescent Hospital Camps.

3	Administration.

4	Appointment.
	    A. Officials.
	    B. Subordinate Officials.

5	Discipline and Control.

6	Correspondence.
	    A. Letters.
	    B. Telegrams.

7	Record Office.
8	Documents.
9	Allotment of Numbers.
10	Return of Strength.
11	Establishments.
12	Promotions.
13	Exchanges and Postings.

14	Movement of Personnel.
	    A. Mobile Branch at Home.
	    B. Mobile Branch Overseas.
	    C. Immobile Branch.

15	Discharges.
	    A. Notice of Discharge.
	    B. On Medical Grounds.
	    C. For Inefficiency.
	    D. On Compassionate Grounds.

(14680.)   Wt. W 2606—G 233. 20m. 5/18. D & S. **G.**

Paragraph.	

15	Discharges—*continued.*
	   E. For Misconduct or Breach of Conditions.
	   F. On Termination of Engagement by Notice.
	   G. Immobile Members.
	   H. Character Certificate.
	   J. Silver Badge.

16	Redress.

17	Leave.
	   A. With Pay.
	   B. Without Pay.
	   C. Absence without Leave.
	   D. Leave of Absence Pass.

18	Travelling Facilities.
	   A. Authority for Movements on Duty.
	   B. Class of Accommodation.
	   C. Use of Warrants.
	   D. Issue of Warrants.
	   E. Travelling Expenses prior to Enrolment, on Joining and on Termination of Service.
	   F. Motor Cars.
	   G. Cabs.
	   H. Travelling Allowance.
	   I. Travelling Claims.
	   J. Half-fare Railway Vouchers.
	   K. The Standard Meal, at Home.
	   L. Hotel Charges.

19	Uniform and Outfit.
	   A. Issue.
	   B. Supply.
	   C. Shoulder Strap Colours.
	   D. Accounting.
	   E. Repairs.
	   F. Discharged Member's Uniform.
	   G. Identity Discs.
	   H. Corps Colours.
	   J. Disposal of Civilian Garments.
	   K. Monthly Return of Stocks.
	   L. Part-worn Garments.

20	Uniforms Rendered Useless.
	   A. General Rules.
	   B. Through the Member's Fault.
	   C. Not through Member's Fault.
	   D. Overseas.

21	Pay.
	   A. Basis of.
	   B. Gratuity for Members of the Mobile Branch.
	   C. Rates of Pay.
	   D. Transfers and Authority for Fixing Rates of Pay.

Paragraph.	

21	Pay—*continued*.
	    E. Issue of Pay.
	    F. Advance of Pay.
	    G. Deductions from Pay.
	    H. Additional Categories.
	    J. Method of Accounting.

22	Accommodation.
	    A. Works Services.
	    B. Officials and Members other than those Officials whose enrolment does not include free quarters.
	    C. Receiving Depôts and Quarters.
	    D. Washing Household Linen.
	    E. Contingent Allowance.
	    F. Barrack Damages, etc.
	    G. Approved Lodgings at Home.
	    H. Hutments.
	    J. Arrangements for Officials and Members in Summer Camps.

23	Board, Lodging, Service and Washing.
24	Fuel and Light Allowances.
25	Rations at Home and Overseas.
26	Ration and Lodging Allowance.
27	Deductions During Leave.
28	Regimental Institutes.
29	Spiritual Ministration.
30	Funerals.

31	Women's Legion.
	    A. Motor Transport Section.
	    B. Military Cookery Section.

32	Re-enrolment of certain existing Personnel of the Q.M.A.A.C. into the Mobile Branch only.

PART II.

RECRUITING.

General Instructions.

33	Provision of Women.

34	Reserved Occupations.
	    A. Debarred from Enrolment.
	    B. Temporarily Debarred from Enrolment.

35	Aliens.
36	Advertisements.
37	Enrolment Form.
38	Enrolment.

Paragraph.	—
39	Special Instructions for Enrolment into the Mobile Branch. A. Enrolment for. B. Controller of Personnel and Recruiting Controllers. C. Method of Indenting. D. Duties of a Recruiting Controller. E. Ministry of Labour. F. Medical Boards. G. Travelling Expenses prior to Enrolment, on Joining and on Termination of Engagement.
40	Special Instructions for Enrolment of Women, except those already employed with the Army, into Immobile Branch.
41	Special Instructions. Enrolment of Women already Employed with the Army into either the Mobile or Immobile Branch. A. Mobile Branch. B. Immobile Branch.

PART III.

MEDICAL SERVICES.

42	Organization.
43	Controllers of Medical Services, Q.M.A.A.C. at Home and Overseas.
44	Assistant Medical Controllers at Home and Overseas.
45	Recruiting Medical Controllers.
46	Medical Officials.
47	Rates of Pay.
48	Rates of Pension or Gratuity of Medical Women.
49	Medical Boards.
50	Travelling Allowance.
51	Admission to Hospitals.
52	Sick Leave.
53	Discharges on Medical Grounds.
54	Dental Treatment.
55	Spectacles, Artificial Dentures and Surgical Appliances.
56	Medical Certificates.
57	Motors.
58	Provision of Nurses in Q.M.A.A.C. Depôts and Quarters.
59	Insurance and Pay during Sickness, etc. A. Classification and Eligibility for Insurance.

Paragraph.	—

59	Insurance and Pay during Sickness, etc.—*continued*.
	  B. Injury or Sickness contracted on Service Overseas.
	  C. On Return Sick from Overseas.
	  D. Death following upon Service Overseas.
	  E. Service at Home.
	  F. Drugs, Medical Attendance, etc.
	  G. Admittance to Hospital, Charges. etc.
	  H. Custody of Insurance Cards.
	  J. Courts of Inquiry for Injuries.

60	Arrears of Insurance for Officials and Members.
61	National Insurance Acts (Unemployment).

APPENDICES.

A. Form of Enrolment in the Q.M.A.A.C.
B. Establishments.
C. Equipment for Q.M.A.A.C. Depôts and Quarters.
D. Scale of Rations.
E. Accounting Instructions.
F. Consolidated Returns.
G. Acknowledgment of Enrolment.
H. Nominal Roll.
J. Result of Selection and Medical Boards.
K. Form of Application for Enrolment—Mobile Branch.
L. ,, ,, ,, ,, —Immobile Branch.
M. Receipt Form for Application for Enrolment.
N. Reference Form.
O. Candidate's Form of Summons.
P. Calling-up Notice.
Q. Refusal of Applicant.
R. Application for Officials for Permanent Staff of, and Information concerning the Q.M.A.A.C Quarters in which Members Requisitioned will be Accommodated.
S. Medical Certificate. (Immobile Branch.)
T. Appointment, Transfer, Promotion and Discharge of Officials.
U. Army Forms only applicable to Q.M.A.A.C.
V. Character Certificate.
W. Discharge Certificate.
X. Detailed Instructions as to the Application to Members of the Q.M.A.A.C. of the Scheme framed under the Injuries in War (Compensation Act), 1914 (Session 2).
XA. Instructions as to the Payment of Injury Pay under the Workmen's Compensation Act to Officials and Members of the Q.M.A.A.C. in cases where Women are injured by Accident in the course of their employment at Home.
Y. Q.M.A.A.C. Uniform.
Z. Repair of Shoes.
ZA. Scale of Camp Equipment.
Index.

REGULATIONS
FOR THE QUEEN MARY'S ARMY AUXILIARY CORPS.

PART I.

DEFINITIONS.

The term "Official" includes the grades specified in para. 4 (A).

The term "Subordinate Official" includes the grades specified in para. 4 (B).

The term "Worker" includes other grades of the Q.M.A.A.C.

The term "Members" includes Subordinate Officials and Workers.

The term "O.C." means the Officer Commanding the military formation to which Officials and Members are attached. The term "Quarters" is used in lieu of the former term "Hostel" or "Residential Hostel," and does not include Approved Lodgings, and the term "Receiving Depôt" in lieu of "Receiving Depôt Hostel."

1. *ORGANIZATION.*

The Q.M.A.A.C. consists of two Branches, (A) Mobile, (B) Immobile.

(A) *Mobile Branch.*

The Mobile Branch will consist of Members who enrol, subject to paras. 2, 34 and 35, or who have already enrolled, in the Corps, with a liability to be transferred, as required, in the United Kingdom if enrolled for Home Service only, or in the United Kingdom and Overseas if enrolled for Service at Home and Overseas. The authorized advantages for the Mobile Branch are described in paras. 18 (J) and 21 (B).

(B) *Immobile Branch.*

(i) The Immobile Branch will consist of Members who live at Home and who are required for local employment subject to paras. 2, 34 and 35. Such Members may be permitted to enrol in the Q.M.A.A.C. on the definite understanding that they may continue to live in their homes and are not liable to be transferred to other places. No Immobile Members will be enrolled under Category B (para. 21 (C)).

(ii) The term " live at Home " (*see* (i) above) is only intended to apply to Members who are ordinarily resident in the locality in which they are required to work. Women who propose to come from outside districts, towns, &c , and to take up lodgings or boarding accommodation in any particular locality for the express purpose of joining the Q.M.A.A.C. Immobile Branch in that locality, are not to be accepted. Such women must enrol in the Mobile Branch and be dealt with accordingly.

2. OBJECT.

(A) *General Substitution.*

The object of the Corps is to effect substitution of women for soldiers in certain employments throughout units, formations and offices administered by the Army Council—other than those specified in para. 34—at Home, and Overseas in such localities as may be directed by G.H.Q. The main categories of employments in which it is intended gradually to effect substitution of Q.M.A.A.C. Members for soldiers at Home and Overseas are indicated in para. 21 (C).

(B) *Motor Drivers Overseas.*

Women Motor Drivers for service Overseas will be provided by the Q.M.A.A.C., except in the case of Motor Ambulance Drivers when they will be found by the General Service Section of the V.A.D.

(C) *Proportionate Substitution.*

The following rules regarding the employment of Members of the Q.M.A.A.C. will be strictly adhered to for calculating the numbers to be employed:—

(i) *Clerical Workers.*—Four clerical workers will be considered as equivalent to three soldier clerks.

(ii) *Technical Workers.*—Four technical workers will be considered as equivalent to three technical soldiers. This also applies to Bakers, para. 21 (C) " F " 2 (c).

(iii) *Other Workers.*—Except as detailed in (i) and (ii) above, and in cases where the employment of a soldier would otherwise have been officially authorized, no Member of the Q.M.A.A.C. will be employed unless a soldier is thereby relieved for other purposes.

(iv) *Relief of N.C.Os.*—In cases where Members of the Q.M.A.A.C. are employed, competent Forewomen will, if possible, replace N.C.Os.

(D) *Substitution at Home.*

Substitution at Home is being gradually introduced by means of the Q.M.A.A.C. into:—

(i) Command employments.

(ii) Garrison employments.

(iii) Regimental employments (*vide* Appendix B) in Reserve and Home Service Units (other than Units in the Home Service Divisions, Mixed and Cyclist Brigades, Graduated Battalions in the Home Service Divisions are, however, allowed women cooks according to approved scale).

(iv) Certain technical employments.

(E) *Conditions of Substitution.*

Substitution will not be undertaken by the Q.M.A.A.C.—

(i) until suitable accommodation is ready for occupation (*see* para. 22),

(ii) until the requisite staff for Quarters is in residence.

(F) *Substitution in Convalescent Hospital Camps.*

Women employed in Convalescent Hospital Camps will only be provided by the Q.M.A.A.C. where combatant soldiers would normally be employed, or where the duties of R.A.M.C. soldiers can be conveniently undertaken by women.

3 ADMINISTRATION.

The Q.M.A.A.C. is administered by a Chief Controller who is responsible to the Adjutant-General for the general administration of the Corps.

4. APPOINTMENT.

(A) *Officials.*—The following grades of Officials are authorized:—

Grade.	Appointment.	Proposed Badge.	Employment.
I.	Chief Controller	1 Double Rose and 1 Rose	H.Q., Q.M.A.A.C.
II.	Chief Controller (Overseas) Deputy Chief Controller	1 Double Rose	H.Q., Q.M.A.A.C.(Overseas). H.Q., Q.M.A.A.C.
III.	Asst. Chief Controller Deputy Chief Controller (Overseas) Controller	1 Fleur-de-lys and 2 Roses	H.Q., Q.M.A.A.C. H.Q., Q.M.A.A.C. (Overseas.) Attached H.Q. certain Commands at Home.
IV.	Deputy Asst. Chief Controller Deputy Controller	1 Fleur-de-lys and 1 Rose	H.Q., Q.M.A.A.C. Attached certain Areas within Commands at Home and to certain Areas Overseas.
V.	Recruiting Controller †Unit Administrator	1 Fleur-de-lys	Attached certain Recruiting Areas at Home. Depôts or Quarters over 500.
VI.	†Unit Administrator Quartermistress	3 Roses	Depôts or Quarters under 500. Certain large Depôts or Quarters.
VII.	†Deputy Administrator Asst. Quartermistress	2 Roses	Depôts or Quarters Staff.
VIII.	†Asst. Administrator	1 Rose	Depôts or Quarters Staff.

† When necessary these appointments may be temporary under **War** Office Orders.

(i) Application Form A.F. W. 3662 (formerly A.G. XI/194) for use by Candidates for these appointments can be obtained through the usual channels.

(ii) Candidates will be required to undergo a short period of probation during which they will receive pay. When this is completed, and if their appointments are finally approved, they will appear in the "London Gazette." For further procedure regarding these appointments, *see* Appendix T.

(iii) All Officials are required to join the Mobile Branch.

(iv) *Officials for Domestic Duties.*

>Officials will be responsible to the O.C. the Units concerned for all Members employed on domestic services under his orders, whether at work or in Quarters. In Quarters where there is more than one Official, the Senior Official may make one of the Junior Officials specifically responsible for this service. In exceptional cases where the number of Members employed on domestic duties is large, application may be made to the War Office for one or more additional Assistant Administrators for this purpose.

(v) *Officials for Technical Duties.*

>(a) In Offices and Workshops where very large numbers of the Q.M.A.A.C. are employed in clerical duties or in technical employments, application may be made, as above, to the War Office for such additional Assistant Administrators as may be required for technical and welfare supervisory duties. Such Officials will be specially selected, and will be whole time skilled persons. It should be stated in the application what technical position it is proposed that these Officials should fill. They will be responsible to the O.C. for the discipline of the Members whilst on duty. The usual conditions as regards residence in Q.M.A.A.C. Quarters will apply, but they will have no duties in the Quarters.

>(b) In Offices and Workshops where the number employed is small, the Senior Official concerned, or an Official deputed by her, will be responsible to the O.C. for the welfare of the Members whilst at work.

(B) *Subordinate Officials.*—The following grades of Subordinate Officials are authorized:—

Grade.	Distinction.	How Worn.
Forewoman	1 Rose, 1 Laurel Wreath	On Right Upper Arm.
Assistant Forewoman	1 Laurel Wreath	,, ,, ,, ,,

(i) Workers will be recommended for promotion by the O.C., with the approval of the Official concerned (as laid down in para. 12).

(ii) Acting Assistant Forewomen (without pay) may be appointed when desired by an O.C. with the approval of the Official concerned.

This acting grade can be removed by an O.C., with the approval of the Official concerned, at any time, and it will automatically lapse if the Member is transferred to another Unit. Such acting Subordinate Officials will wear the badge as laid down for Assistant Forewomen above.

5. DISCIPLINE AND CONTROL.

(*a*) Os.C. will afford every facility for the proper discharge of their duty to all grades of Officials and Subordinate Officials, who are responsible for supervision and who will bring to the notice of such Os.C. any irregularities that may occur. The supervisory duties will include all questions concerning the welfare and comfort of Members whilst away from their Quarters and at work.

(*b*) Officials and Members, whilst on duty away from their Quarters, will be under the orders of the O.C. the Unit to which they are attached for duty. The instructions of the O.C. will be conveyed to Members through the Official or Subordinate Official supervising the particular services in which the Members are employed. Whilst off duty, or on duty in their Quarters, Members will be under the orders of Officials of the Q.M.A.A.C.

(*c*) The granting of leave of absence and other privileges may be postponed or restricted at the discretion of the Official concerned in the case of Members who commit breaches of discipline.

(*d*) Breaches of discipline which cannot be dealt with under (*c*) above will be reported by the Official or Subordinate Official concerned, to the O.C., who may deal with the same by the infliction of fines as laid down in para. 14 of Army Form W. 3578 (Enrolment Form, Appendix A.).

(e) When in the opinion of the O.C. a case cannot be adequately disposed of under (c) above or by the infliction of a fine under (d), he will obtain statements of witnesses in writing and forward them without delay with a full report to higher military authority for decision.

(f) When a case is referred under (e) to higher military authority the General Officer to whom the case is referred may decide either to:—

    (i) Refer the case back to the O.C. for disposal under (d) above or

    (ii) In the case of a Member serving at Home inform the Civil Police with a view to a prosecution or to proceedings under Defence of the Realm Regulation 42 (c), or

    (iii) Forward the case to the G.O.C.-in-C. or G.O.C. with his recommendations, which may include a recommendation that the Member be discharged under para 15 (E).

6. CORRESPONDENCE.

(A) *Letters.*

Official correspondence on all questions relating to the Q.M.A.A.C. will be carried out through the usual Army channels, both at Home and Overseas, and will be registered in A.B. 193.

(B) *Telegrams.*

(i) Inland telegrams, on official business, may be despatched without prepayment by all Officials of the Q.M.A.A.C.

(ii) Each telegram will be certified as on War Office business, with the signature of the Official, and description of appointment, followed by the initials "Q.M.A.A.C."

7. RECORD OFFICE.

A Record Office for the Q.M.A.A.C. has been established with Headquarters in London, and a Record Section has been established Overseas.

8. DOCUMENTS.

All records of service affecting movements of Members, changes of category, or rates of pay, will be notified in Part II. Orders (A.F. O. 1810).

(A) All casualties will be recorded on a separate A.F. O. 1810 by the Accounting Unit (*i.e.*, units with which Q.M.A.A.C.

are employed or * Receiving Depôts). The permanent staff of Quarters will be shown in Part II. Orders of the unit to which they are attached for pay. Copies will be forwarded to Command Paymasters concerned and to the Officer i/c Q.M.A.A.C. Records, London, as follows:—

    (i) From O.C. Units, one weekly copy showing all casualties. Great care will be exercised that casualties to Officials and Members are not included in Part II. Orders for soldiers.

    (ii) From Receiving Depôts, one copy on Mondays, Wednesdays, and Fridays, showing all Casualties.

    (iii) All Part II. Orders will be numbered in sequence. Those forwarded by units will be numbered in a separate series marked Q.M.A.A.C. The numbers will commence at 1 on the 1st January of each year. When more than one sheet of Orders are issued on any given day the words "First Sheet" will be inserted at the top of the first sheet, and the words "Second Sheet" at the top of the second sheet, and so on; the last sheet in such cases will have the words "Last Sheet" inserted at the top.

(B) A.F. B. 103 (Casualty Form) will be rendered as follows:

    (i) In the case of Members proceeding Overseas, A.F. B. 103 and nominal rolls will be prepared in accordance with existing instructions and sent to the Officer i/c Q.M.A.A.C. Records, who will forward them Overseas.

    (ii) In the case of Members enrolled by the O.C. a unit stationed at Home, A.F. B. 103 will be prepared by the Officer i/c Q.M.A.A.C. Records and forwarded to him.

    (iii) In the case of Members enrolled by a Selection Board A.F. B. 103 will be prepared by the Q.M.A.A.C. Official of the Receiving Depôt to which the Member is posted.

    (iv) Punishments inflicted under paras. 13 and 14 of the Enrolment Form will be recorded in A.F. B. 103.

(C) A.F. B. 178 will be rendered as follows:—

    (i) A.F. B. 178, Table 1 of which will be varied to agree with the particulars given in A.F. W. 3577 (Identification Certificate), will be prepared by the Medical Board in accordance with existing instructions and retained by the Officer i/c Q.M.A.A.C. Records.

---

* Officials in charge of Quarters other than Depôts will on no account render Part II. Orders.

(ii) In the case of Members enrolled by an O.C. a unit A.F. B. 178, Table 1 of which will be varied as in (i) above, will be prepared by the Officer i/c Q.M.A.A.C. Records.

(D) A.B. 64 and A.F. W. 3577:

Every Member proceeding Overseas will be in possession of A.B. 64 (Pay Book) and A.F. W. 3577 (Identification Certificate).

9 *ALLOTMENT OF NUMBERS.*

On receipt of Part II. Orders, as detailed in para. 8, the Officer i/c Q.M.A.A.C. Records will allot numbers as follows: —

- (a) For Mobile Members a roll showing numbers so allotted will be forwarded to the Official of the Receiving Depôt concerned.
- (b) For Immobile Members to the O.C. to whom they are attached.
- (c) He will also forward a copy of the roll to the Command Paymaster of the Command in which the Receiving Depôts or the Units are situated.
- (d) All Corps numbers when allotted must be published in Part II. Orders.

10. *RETURN OF STRENGTH.*

(a) All units employing Officials and Members will render to the Officer i/c Q.M.A.A.C. Records a monthly return A.F. W. 3968 in duplicate showing by categories: —

- (i) All Officials and Members employed (*see* para. 21 (C)).
- (ii) The number of soldiers who have been replaced by Members.
- (iii) The number of soldiers still employed and replaceable by women.

11. *ESTABLISHMENTS.*

Details of Establishments will be found in Appendix B.

12. *PROMOTIONS.*

(a) Officials will make a point of bringing to the notice of Os.C. concerned Workers who prove themselves worthy of promotion to the grade of Forewomen. (Para. 4 (B).)

(b) Recommendations for such promotions will be made in writing by the O.C. with the approval of the Official concerned; if at Home, to the Officer i/c Q.M.A.A.C. Records direct, and if Overseas, to the Official G.H.Q.

(c) The Officer i/c Q.M.A.A.C. Records and G.H.Q. (Overseas) will each keep nominal rolls by categories of such Workers, according to their date of recommendation. As a vacancy for promotion to grade of Forewoman occurs, the O.C. will apply to the Officer i/c Q.M.A.A.C. Records or to G.H.Q. (Overseas), who will make the appointment from the category of employment required to fill the vacancy, and will authorize the move if necessary.

(d) If a Member who is recommended for promotion is transferred from Service at Home to Service Overseas, or *vice versâ*, notification of the fact, with the date of recommendation, will be exchanged between the Officer i/c Q.M.A.A.C. Records and G.H.Q. (Overseas).

(e) Promotions to Assistant Forewomen, according to the scale laid down, will be made by the O.C., with the approval of the Official concerned, and without reference either to the Officer i/c Q.M.A.A.C. Records or to G.H.Q. (Overseas).

(f) All such promotions will be notified in Part II. Orders.

13. *EXCHANGES AND POSTING.*

(a) Members who desire to exchange from the Immobile to the Mobile Branch will, if recommended by the O.C. and Official concerned, and after examination by a Medical Board, be referred to the Officer i/c Q.M.A.A.C. Records direct for decision. If the Member is not working directly under any Official of the Corps, she will also appear before a Q.M.A.A.C. Selection Board, who will decide as to the suitability of her exchange. The Recruiting Controller should obtain her references from the Officer i/c Q.M.A.A.C. Records.

(b) Members who desire to exchange from the Mobile to the Immobile Branch will, if recommended by the O.C. and Official concerned, be referred to the Officer i/c Q.M.A.A.C. Records direct for decision (*see* para. 1 (B)).

(c) Recommendation by a Medical Board at Home for posting a Member while on leave from service Overseas to service at Home for reasons of health, or recommendation on medical grounds for transfer of a Member from General Service to Home Service only, or *vice versâ*, will be submitted to the Officer i/c Q.M.A.A.C. Records by the President of the Medical Board.

14. *MOVEMENTS OF PERSONNEL.*

(A) *Mobile Branch at Home.*

(i) Units moving to new stations, whether the move is within one Command Area or not, will take their Q.M.A.A.C. personnel with them.

(ii) Before such moves are ordered, Headquarters of Commands will ascertain through the Controller whether suitable accommodation at the new station is available and ready for occupation.
(iii) If there is no accommodation available, the personnel will be left behind, and will be allotted to other units under the orders of Command Headquarters.
(iv) Exceptionally, in the case of an exchange of quarters between two units having approximately the same establishment of Q.M.A.A.C. personnel, the relieving units will take over each other's personnel.
(v) The Q.M.A.A.C. Mobile personnel will be moved in the above cases by the military authority who orders the move of the unit.
(vi) Moves of individual Mobile Members for welfare purposes, other than on promotion, if recommended by the O.C. or Official concerned, will be submitted for approval to Command Headquarters. If it is necessary to move a Member for these purposes from one Command to another, the move may be authorized and carried out by the Headquarters of the Commands concerned. Such transfers will only be recommended in very exceptional cases.
(vii) If for any reason a surplus of Mobile Members are unemployed at a station, and there is no immediate likelihood of employing them, they will be moved by Command Headquarters to the nearest Receiving Depôt in the Command for re-posting to units.
(viii) Reposting of Members on promotion will be ordered by the Officer i/c Q.M.A.A.C. Records or G.H.Q. (Overseas) in accordance with para. 12.
(ix) All Members returning from Service Overseas to Service at Home will pass through the Receiving Depôts for Overseas.
(x) Motor Drivers returned from Overseas permanently fit for service at Home only will be given the opportunity of transferring to the Women's Legion, Motor Transport Section.

(B) *Mobile Branch Overseas.*

All movements of personnel Overseas will be authorized by the C.C. Overseas under the orders of G.H.Q.

(C) *Immobile Branch.*

(i) Members of the Immobile Branch who may change their permanent homes can apply to be transferred, within their Branch, to another town and will be dealt with as under (vi) of (A) above.

(ii) If a unit employing Members of the Immobile Branch changes station, the Members will be held to serve with the incoming unit, or if not required, they will be given one week's notice, in accordance with para. 37 (c). In such circumstances, however, Members will always be given the option of transfer to the Mobile Branch (*see* para. 13 (a)).

15. DISCHARGES.

(A) *Notice of Discharge.*

(i) In all cases of discharge except under (D) and (E) below, Members will be given one month's or one week's notice according to the condition of their respective enrolment (para 16 of A.F. W. 3578, see Appendix A) by the O.C. the unit to which the Members are attached for duty, through the Officials concerned, from the date on which the discharge is authorized. All discharges will be notified in Part II. Orders.

(ii) Members, who are serving Overseas, and who are recommended for discharge, will be transferred Home for final settlement and discharge to the Receiving Depôt for Overseas.

(B) *On Medical Grounds.*

For discharges on medical grounds, *see* para. 53.

(C) *For Inefficiency.*

Applications for discharge on the grounds of inefficiency may be forwarded by the O.C. to the Command Headquarters or to G.H.Q. Overseas for approval. The O.C. and Official concerned will endorse their recommendation thereon, the Member being retained with the unit pending disposal.

(D) *On Compassionate Grounds.*

Applications for discharge on compassionate grounds, with the recommendations of the O.C. and the Official concerned, will receive sympathetic consideration. These will be forwarded to the Command Headquarters concerned for approval, or in the case of Members serving Overseas to the Officer i/c Q.M.A.A.C. Records, London, together with a detailed report showing that the fullest investigation has been made. The O.C. will use his discretion as to granting immediate leave pending a decision as above. The O.C. will as a rule refer such cases for investigation by the local Police before taking action. If the application is agreed to there will be no pay beyond the last day of service. Before granting a discharge care will be taken to ascertain if the grounds on which the application is made cannot be met by granting leave under para. 17.

(E) *For Misconduct or Breach of Conditions.*

(i) Members will not be discharged for misconduct or breach of conditions (para. 16 of A.F. W. 3578, *see* Appendix A) without the authority of the Army Council or any General Officer authorized by them.

(ii) Those serving at Home will be reported to the O.C. and the Official concerned, thence through the usual Military channels for decision as in (i) above.

(iii) Those serving Overseas, who commit *serious* offences, will be returned to England for disposal. In such cases a report from the Chief Controller Overseas will be attached to the official communication to the War Office for the information of the Chief Controller Q.M.A.A.C.

(iv) Members of the Mobile Branch charged with *serious* misconduct, when serving at Home, will be sent to the nearest Receiving Depôt pending settlement.

(v) On receipt of authority for discharge, the Member's pay will cease from the date of discharge.

(F) *On Termination of Engagement by Notice.*

(i) Discharges on termination of engagement by notice will only be made by Command Headquarters concerned when Members of a specific Category or Sub-Category are surplus to requirements.

(ii) Such Members will first be given the option of transferring to another category, *see* 21 D. (iv).

(iii) If such Members are unwilling to transfer, the matter must be referred to the War Office in order to ascertain if they cannot be absorbed in the same Category or Sub-Category elsewhere.

(G) *Immobile Members.*

In the case of Immobile Members where no Official is available the O.C. will take the necessary action.

(H) *Character Certificate.* (A.F. W. 3677. *See* Appendix V.)

(i) After a discharge has been sanctioned and on its being notified in Part II Orders, the Officer i/c Q.M.A.A.C. Records will complete the Discharge Certificate (Appendix W). The cause of discharge will be shown as follows:—

(a) For inefficiency.
(b) On compassionate grounds.
(c) Medically unfit.
(d) For misconduct.
(e) On termination of engagement.

(ii) After a discharge has been carried out by the Officer i/c Q.M.A.A.C. Records, he will forward the completed Discharge

Certificate, together with the Character Certificate, Army Form W. 3677 (Appendix V), in blank to the O.C. who notifies the Member's discharge, or in the case of the staff of Depôt or Quarters to the Official concerned. Normally, the Member's character at work (Part II) will be filled in by the O.C., and her personal character (Part. III) by the Official concerned. If no Official is available the O.C. will complete both parts of the certificate.

(iii) The Member's character will be assessed generally on the lines laid down in paras. 417 and 418 King's Regulations as for soldiers. The guiding principle, while being fair to her prospective employer, is to help a Member to secure employment. To this end, distinction will be made between Parts II and III of the Character Certificate. Part II relates to her efficiency, and Part III to her personal character whilst employed with the Q.M.A.A.C.

(J.) *Silver Badge.*

The Silver Badge may be issued, on recommendation, to Officials and Members who are discharged by a Medical Board as permanently unfit for further service in the Corps. Application will be made by the Official or Member concerned to the Officer i/c Q.M.A.A.C. Records.

16. *REDRESS.*

Any Official or Member who feels aggrieved, or considers that she has been unjustly treated by her superior, may submit her case in writing through the Superior Official under whom she serves for investigation. All such complaints will be forwarded by the Official concerned through the O.C. and the usual Military channels, for decision by the G.O.C.-in-C. or G.O.C., or by the Army Council when necessary.

17. *LEAVE.*

(A) *With Pay.*

(i) Officials or Members serving at Home or Overseas will be allowed a fortnight's leave with pay during each year's service, provided the exigencies of the service will permit, and in the case of those serving in France, free transport will be granted them to their homes in the United Kingdom and back to France. Free travelling facilities for leave from France will not under any circumstances be granted more than once in six months. Members of Category B (Mobile Branch) when on paid leave will receive pay as laid down in para. 26 (b)

(ii) Four days' leave with pay, which will not be reckoned in the fortnight's leave, will be granted, as in (i) above, prior to embarkation, to all Members for service at Home or Overseas who are ultimately drafted Overseas after they have served at Home. This leave does not apply to those who, after enrolment, are posted direct to a Receiving Depôt prior to embarkation, but only to Members who have served at Home.

(B) *Without Pay.*

(i) Unpaid leave up to one month, in excess of the paid leave provided for in (A) above may be granted to Officials or Members employed on service at Home, at the discretion of the O.C. in consultation with the Official concerned, in cases of urgent private affairs.

(ii) Applications for unpaid leave in excess of one month should be referred to the Officer i/c Q.M.A.A.C. Records, with the recommendation of the O.C. and Official concerned endorsed thereon. Such leave will be notified in Part II Orders.

(iii) Applications for unpaid leave under the terms of this paragraph should only be considered under exceptional circumstances, and the period of leave granted cannot be recorded as service, nor reckoned for gratuity under para. 21 (B).

(iv) In the case of Officials or Members serving Overseas, all applications for unpaid leave as above will be submitted for sanction to General Headquarters. Unless they are entitled to free warrants as above they will be required to pay their own fare.

(C) *Absence Without Leave.*

Instructions with regard to absence without leave have been issued separately to those concerned.

(D) *Leave of Absence Pass.*

(i) A leave of absence pass for Members serving at Home, A.F. W. 3675, has been approved.

(ii) It will be issued when a Member is proceeding on leave extending over 12 hours, and must on demand be shown to an Official or Subordinate Official.

(iii) No officer or soldier of H.M. Forces is authorized to demand or examine it.

(iv) *Mobile Branch.*—A Member will be granted leave by the O.C., with the concurrence of the Official concerned, or, in the case of a Receiving Depôt, by the Official concerned. but in all cases the pass will be issued and signed by an Official.

(v) *Immobile Branch.*—The same procedure will be followed but in cases where no Official is available, the O.C. will himself issue and sign the pass.

(E) Sick Leave. *See* para. 52.

18. *TRAVELLING FACILITIES.*

(A) Authority for movements on duty may be given for:—

(i) *Officials by:—*
  (a) Chief Controller.
  (b) Deputy Chief Controller.
  (c) Controller of Medical Services.
  (d) Controllers.
  (e) Deputy Controllers.
  (f) Recruiting Controllers.
  (g) Unit Administrators of Receiving Depôts or their deputies in case of absence.

(ii) *Members by:—*
  (a) Controllers.
  (b) Deputy Controllers.
  (c) Recruiting Controllers.
  (d) Unit Administrators of Receiving Depôts or their deputies in case of absence.
  (e) Deputy Controller or the Senior Official at Stations Overseas.

(iii) *In all cases by :—*

The O.C. to whom the Official or Member is attached for duty.

(B) *Class of Accommodation.*

When travelling at the public expense, railway accommodation is admissible as follows:—
  (i) Officials—First class.
  (ii) Members—Third class.

(C) *Use of Warrants.*
  (i) Officials, when travelling on duty in uniform will use A.B. 205.
  (ii) Members, when travelling on duty in uniform, will use A.B. 422.
  (iii) When Officials and Members not in uniform are ordered to travel by rail on duty, warrants will not be issued, but their tickets will be purchased for them from imprest account by the O.C. or the Official of the Receiving Depôt concerned.

(D) *Issue of Warrants.*

Warrants must as a general rule be issued and signed by an officer, but exceptionally the following Officials

are authorized to issue and sign A.B. 205 and A.B. 422:—
- (i) The Chief Controller, or her deputy in case of absence.
- (ii) Controller of Medical Services.
- (iii) Controllers at Headquarters.
- (iv) Recruiting Controllers.
- (v) The Unit Administrators of Receiving Depôts or their deputies in case of absence.

(E) *Travelling Expenses prior to Enrolment on Joining and on Termination of Service.*

(i) *Officials.*—Officials are not entitled to travel at the public expense.
- (a) For attendance at a Selection or Medical Board before enrolment.
- (b) On joining for duty.
- (c) They are entitled during the period of the war and on general demobilization to travelling expenses to their homes in the United Kingdom on satisfactory termination of their engagement.

(ii) *Members:—*
- (a) Return railway warrants will be issued, by the Officers of the Ministry of Labour, to applicants residing more than five miles from the place of a Selection Board.
- (b) A further warrant will be issued by the local Officer of the Ministry of Labour when calling up enrolled Members for duty.
- (c) A railway warrant will be issued to their homes in the United Kingdom on satisfactory termination of their engagement.

(F) *Motor Cars.*
G.Os.C.-in-C. or the G.O.C. are authorized to provide motor-cars from the "pool" of vehicles posted to Command Headquarters, when considered necessary, in cases where existing railway or other facilities do not enable the duties of Controllers to be efficiently carried out.

(G) *Cabs.*
Members will not be entitled to claim a refund for cab fares.

(H) *Travelling Allowance.*

(i) Travelling allowance at the following rates are authorized for journeys on duty:—

Rate 1.	Rate 2.	Rate 3.	Rate 4.
When absent at night for a period not exceeding 14 nights in one place.	After 14 nights in one place or for the whole period if it was known before starting that the stay in one place must exceed 14 nights.	When absent above 10 hours but not absent for a night.	For the day of return from a journey which exceeds 24 hours, provided the journey is completed later than 7 a.m.
(*a*) 15*s*. nightly	10*s*. nightly	5*s*. ...	3*s*. 6*d*.
(*b*) 10*s*. nightly	7*s*. 6*d*. nightly	3*s*. 6*d*. ...	3*s*. 6*d*.
(*c*) 5*s*. nightly	3*s*. 4*d*. nightly	1*s*. 8*d*. ...	1*s*. 8*d*.

These rates are applicable as follows:—

(*a*) To Officials in receipt of salaries of £150 per annum or over, including those Officials whose pay together with the value of free quarters equals or exceeds £150 per annum.
(*b*) To Officials other than under (*a*).
(*c*) To Members.

(ii) Travelling allowance will not be issuable for nights when food and accommodation are provided in kind at the public expense.

(iii) The daily rate of travelling allowance will not be issuable when arrangements are made for the provision of food at the public expense.

(iv) Normally, travelling allowance will not be issuable for a stay of more than 14 nights in one place. In exceptional circumstances the allowance may be continued beyond that period, if authorized by the G.O.C.-in-C. or G.O.C of the Command in which the detention takes place, a suitable rate being fixed by the War Office within the limit of Rate 2 to meet any extra expense to which the Member may be put.

(v) Travelling allowance will not be issuable for journeys of less than four miles from Headquarters, on first appointment, on termination of engagement, or whilst on board ship and messed at the public expense.

(vi) The rates issuable in places outside the United Kingdom will be published in Local Routine Orders.

(vii) The rates of travelling allowance, and the conditions under which they are issuable, are subject to alteration.

(viii) Allowances at Rate 1 are issuable subject to (ii) above, to Officials and Members proceeding to France on short visits not exceeding twenty-seven consecutive nights.

The allowance may be increased by 2s. 6d. for each night spent on duty in Paris.

Any such allowances will be claimed in the ordinary way at Home.

(ix) Officials and Members whose stay in France exceeds twenty-seven consecutive nights will be granted the allowances admissible for Officials and Members stationed there, which are based on the Home rates.

These allowances will be claimed from the Command Paymaster, Base, British Armies in France.

(I) *Travelling Claims.*

Travelling claims (A.F. O. 1771) for Officials or Members travelling on duty can be certified as performed on the public service by the Official or O.C. authorizing the journey, and will be submitted for payment to the Command Paymaster of the Command in which the claimant is stationed.

(J) *Half-fare Railway Vouchers. Mobile Branch only.*

(i) Arrangements have been made by which a railway concession voucher (R.E.C. 35) may be issued once every six months to Officials and Members when travelling in uniform on leave.

(ii) The voucher entitles the holder to a third class return journey at single fare (1917 rate). These vouchers for the use of those referred to in (i) above have been endorsed with the letters "Q.M.A.A.C." in red. The reduced fare must be paid, and the voucher exchanged for a ticket at the booking office.

(iii) Each voucher must bear the stamp of the issuing office, be properly completed in ink, and signed in manuscript by the issuing Authority, and by the individual to whom it is issued. The counterfoil must also be completed in all respects.

(iv) No applications for refunds will be entertained in the case of lost vouchers, or of journeys for which a voucher was issuable but was not issued.

(v) Vouchers will be indented for on the War Office by units in the usual way, the number of the form (R.E.C. 35) being invariably quoted.

(vi) Vouchers will be issued to Officials and Members by:—
   (a) Os.C. units to which they are attached for duty.
   (b) Controllers of the Q.M.A.A.C.
   (c) Senior Officials of Receiving Depôt.

(K) *The Standard Meal; at Home.*

The standard meal will be supplied at railway station refreshment rooms, when open, to individual Officials or Members, and to small parties, on payment in cash of 1s. per head.

(L) *Hotel Charges.*

The facilities for reduced charges for officers at Hotels, Boarding Houses, Restaurants, and other places have been extended to include Officials.

Lists of Hotels and Prices will be found at local Military Headquarters, and at local Railway Stations, for reference by all concerned. The prices are fixed at from 10 per cent. to 20 per cent. below the usual prices ruling in the locality.

19. *UNIFORM AND OUTFIT.*

The supply of uniform as from 1st April, 1918, inclusive, will be as follows:—

Receiving Depôts will report to the Deputy Assistant Chief Controller (Clothing) the exact stocks of garments held on charge by them as at midnight, March 31st–April 1st, 1918, accompanied by a nominal roll of women for whom grants in money are due from the Command Paymaster prior to 1st April, 1918. This nominal roll will show the amounts due, and the dates upon which the amounts became due. The grants due from Command Paymasters will not now be paid.

(A) *Issue.*

(i) A sealed pattern of uniform has been approved, and will be worn by all grades serving Overseas.

(ii) Uniform will only be worn at Home by those grades whose duties necessitate regular attendance at camps or other military formations, and the issue thereof will be limited accordingly.

(iii) Officials entitled to wear uniform will draw an outfit allowance of £20 from the Command Paymaster who makes the first issue of pay. No additional grant will be allowed in respect of upkeep, and no free issue of garments or issues on repayment will be made to Officials.

(iv) Members entitled to wear uniform will receive an annual issue of stated garments. Further garments necessitated by the special nature of a Member's work will be issuable conditionally at the discretion of the G.O.C.-in-C. or G.O.C. of the Command in which she is serving at home, or the F.M.C.-in-C., France.

(v) A renewal grant, as shown in Appendix Y, will be issuable at the commencement of the second six months of each year's service to each Member entitled to wear uniform, and will be credited to the Member through the Pay List.

(vi) Garments issued to Members free will be the property of the State. With the exception of greatcoats, badges and brassards, of which only an initial issue is allowed, Members will be allowed to hold on charge garments amounting to 2 complete free Annual issues of such garments as have been issued to them in their free Annual Issues. Garments in excess of this quantity will be returned by the O.C. to the nearest Receiving Depôt.

After two free annual issues have been made, additional free issues of garments will only be made in exchange for a similar number of worn garments. All garments returned to Depôts will be cleaned and disposed of as part-worn garment; if unsuitable for this purpose they will be returned to the Deputy Assistant Chief Controller (Clothing) for ultimate disposal.

Garments purchased by Members must be for their own personal use and must remain their own property.

Garments issued as Conditional Issues will be returned by the O.C. to the nearest Receiving Depôt when a Member ceases to be employed on work justifying the issue.

(vii) Such articles of uniform as are normally included in the Annual Issue may be purchased by Members entitled to uniform from Receiving Depôts on repayment. These will be charged against the Members on A.F. W. 3963.

(viii) Free Annual Issues under these Regulations will, where issuable, only be allowed 12 months after the Member's original initial grant became due.

(ix) Members who drew an initial annual grant before 1st October, 1917, will not be allowed either an increased grant or garments which appear as " Annual Issue " in Appendix Y, and are supplementary to those authorized on that date, until 12 months after the original initial grant. Conditional issues may be made at the discretion of G.O.C.-in-C., irrespective of the date of the original initial grant.

(x) Members who drew an initial annual grant after 30th September, 1917, will be allowed such garments shown in Appendix Y as are supplementary to those authorized on that date, and these will be accounted for and renewable as if they had been issued on the date of the original initial grant.

(xi) Immobile Members will be entitled to purchase on payment only such garments as are included in their Annual Issue.

(B) *Supply.*

(i) Each Official will forward her application for her Outfit Allowance to the Command Paymaster, accompanied by Form A.G. XI (1) directing her to take up duty, which will state whether she is to wear uniform or not, and Form A.G. XI (1A), being a certificate to the effect that she has joined for duty. This certificate will be signed by the Official concerned under whom she is directly serving.

(ii) When a Member passes through a Receiving Depôt the initial Annual Issue of garments authorized under Appendix Y will be made by the Receiving Depôt.

(iii) Information as to the necessity for individual Members being provided with uniform on joining will be in the possession of the Official concerned of the Receiving Depôt to which the Members are sent for allocation to their particular duties.

(iv) When a Member joins for duty without passing through a Receiving Depôt, the O.C. will indent on the nearest Receiving Depôt on A.F. W. 3966 for the requisite articles of uniform, certifying as to the necessity for uniform, in accordance with the principle laid down in A (ii) above. The O.C. will also verify that the garments indented for on A.F. W. 3966 can be correctly claimed by the Members concerned.

(v) Subsequent Annual Issues after the initial Annual Issue will be demanded by the O.C. on A.F. W. 3966 from the nearest Receiving Depôt.

(C) *Shoulder Strap Colours.*

(i) The Grades of Officials and Section of Employment will be denoted by a coloured inset in the shoulder strap, as follows:—

H.Q., Q.M.A.A.C. (England and France) Controller Deputy Controller	Blue.
Recruiting Controller	Green.
Unit Administrator Deputy Administrator Assistant Administrator Quartermistress	Orange.
Household Section	Red.
Mechanical Section (except Motor Drivers) Miscellaneous Section	Purple.
Clerical Section	Brown.
Motor Drivers	Claret.

(ii) Q.M.A.A.C. hat badges and shoulder numerals will be worn as part of their uniform by all Grades of the Mobile Branch who are entitled to uniform.

(iii) The Corps badge will be worn on the hat and collar or the coat by all Officials. Grade badges will be worn on the shoulder strap.

(iv) Members transferred from the Women's Legion will be permitted to wear the badge of the Women's Legion in addition to the above.

(D) *Accounting.*

(i) *At Home.*—All garments issuable will be obtained by Receiving Depôts from the Q.M.A.A.C. Clothing Depôt, 124, Charing Cross Road, London, W.C. 2, indents being submitted on A.F. W. 3962. Receiving Depôts will keep a clothing account in Army Book 165, all receipts from the Q.M.A.A.C. Clothing Depôt being supported by a copy of the Clothing Depôt Issue Vouchers. Receiving Depôts will be responsible for the correctness of issues made by them.

(ii) Issues will be supported by A.Fs. W. 3966 or W. 3963. The issues made during each week will be summarized on A.F. W. 3965 for inclusion in A.B. 165.

(iii) Free issues from the Receiving Depôt will be made on A.F. W. 3966, showing the Members' names, &c., and containing their receipts for the garments issued. A certificate that the Member is authorized to wear uniform will be given on the Army Form.

(iv) Issues on payment will be demanded on A.F. W. 3963, one copy of which will be rendered with the pay list in support of the deduction from the Member's pay, a second copy containing a certificate of credit to the public, and the Member's receipt for the articles will be forwarded by the Command Paymaster to the Receiving Depôt.

(v) Current prices of garments will be circulated quarterly to Receiving Depôts by the Deputy Assistant Chief Controller (Clothing), and can be obtained from them on application.

(vi) A combined Clothing History Sheet and Transfer Clothing Statement (A.F. W. 3964) will be kept for each Member and will be transferred with her whenever she changes her station or unit. On it will be recorded all issues of clothing, whether free or on repayment, and all issues of Renewal Grants.

(vii) Renewal Grants will be paid through the Pay List on the authority of the O.C., or, in the case of Members of the Permanent Staff of a Receiving Depôt, by the Official concerned.

(E) *Repairs.*

(i) Facilities will be given in Army Workshops for the repair of boots and shoes for Members of the Mobile Branch on repayment. (*See* Appendix Z.)

Officials will not be granted these facilities.

(ii) Boots and shoes will on no account be repaired in Regimental Workshops, but may be sent by the O.C., or in the case of Depôt Permanent Staffs, by the Official concerned of the Depôt, to the Command Boot Repair Depôt for all repairs, A.F. W. 3963 (suitably amended) being forwarded in triplicate at the same time. Members must make their own arrangements for conveying the boots and shoes to the O.C. or the Official concerned at their own expense. Charges for postage or carriage, &c., for subsequent conveyance to the workshops will be paid for through the Imprest Account of the O.C. or Official concerned, and charged against the public.

(iii) The charges for repairs to boots and shoes will be notified by the Command Boot Repair Depôt to the O.C. or Official of the Receiving Depôt concerned, on A.F. W. 3963, two copies of which will be returned to the Unit or Depôt, for disposal in accordance with D (iv) above.

(iv) Repairs to other articles of uniform will not be carried out in Army Workshops, but will be arranged for by the Members themselves.

(F) *Discharged Member's Uniform.*

The uniform of a Member who ceases to be employed will be sent to the nearest Receiving Depôt by the O.C.

(G) *Identity Discs.*

Identity Discs will be worn by all grades proceeding Overseas.

(H) *Corps Colours.*

(i) The official Corps colours will be blue and white, and will always be worn by Members of the Mobile Branch, as a sealed pattern of brassard (blue with "Q.M.A.A.C." in white letters).

The Immobile Branch will wear the brassard when proceeding to and from their work, and whilst at work.

(ii) On discharge for any reason, the O.C., or, in the case of the Permanent Staff of a Receiving Depôt, the Official concerned will be responsible that the Member's brassard is returned to the nearest Receiving Depôt.

(J) *Disposal of Civilian Garments.*

Members of the Mobile Branch entitled to wear uniform will not be allowed to retain corresponding articles of civilian clothing. As soon as uniform has been issued, such articles will be packed up and addressed by the Member and sent away by the Official concerned, who will pay for the postage through her Imprest Account.

(K) *Monthly Return of Stocks.*

(i) Receiving Depôts will render A.F. W. 3967 to reach the Deputy Assistant Chief Controller (Clothing) on the first of each month.

(L) *Part-worn Garments.*

(i) Part-worn garments returned to Receiving Depôts will be cleaned at public expense and, when available, will be purchaseable, on repayment, by Members at half the cost of a new garment.

20. UNIFORMS RENDERED USELESS.

(A) *General Rules.*

(i) In all cases of uniform being rendered unserviceable owing to an exceptional cause while a Member is on duty, a Board, composed of not less than one Army Officer as President, and two Officials, will be arranged by the Officer Commanding the Army Unit with which the owner of the damaged garment is working, to decide whether the garment has been rendered useless:—

(a) Owing to the fault of the Member; or
(b) Not owing to the fault of the Member.

(ii) If the garment is so damaged as to be obviously unwearable, application will be made by the O.C. of the Army Unit with which the Member works, to the nearest Receiving Depôt at Home, or the Clothing Depôt, Overseas, for a similar garment in substitution. A.F. W. 3963, headed in red ink "Substitution Garment" and giving in the "Remarks" column the date upon which the Member should receive her next annual clothing issue, will be used for this purpose. Application for another garment will be made as soon as possible without waiting for the decision of the Board.

(iii) Whenever possible, the Receiving Depôt will supply a "Part-worn" garment, but should the Depôt have none on charge, a new garment will be supplied.

(iv) Members will be responsible for replacing at their own expense garments rendered useless when they are off duty.

(B) *Through the Member's Fault.*

(i) If available, a part-worn garment will be supplied and half the cost of a new garment will be charged against the Member on A.F. W. 3963. If no part-worn garment is available, a new garment will be supplied, and the cost charged to the Member in the same way. It will be clearly understood that, as the stock of part-worn garments will always fluctuate, no Member can claim a right to be supplied with garments other than new.

(ii) The Receiving Depôt will notify the O.C. the Army Unit concerned of the price of the garment to be paid by the Member.

(C) *Not through the Member's Fault.*

(i) If available, a part-worn garment will be supplied, free of charge, otherwise a new garment.

(ii) Charges against Members for garments supplied in substitution for garments rendered unwearable by the Member's fault will be adjusted in the same manner as for other issues on repayment, *see* 19 (D) (iv) above.

(iii) In all cases the proceedings of the Board will be rendered with A.F. W. 3963 to the Command Paymaster, who will forward it with the certified copy of A.F. W. 3963 to the Receiving Depôt concerned.

(D) *Overseas.*

(i) Renewal Grants, as they become due, will be noted on page 3 of the Pay Book. Credit to the Member's accounts will be given by the Base Paymaster as the grants accrue.

(ii) The instructions given for Clothing Accounting at Home will be carried out Overseas so far as they are applicable. For issues on repayment or in substitution and for charges for repairs to boots, the two copies of A.F. W. 3963 received by the unit from the Depôt, or the Base Boot Repair Depôt, will be sent to the Command Paymaster, Base, for disposal as in 19 (D) (iv) above.

21. *PAY.*

(A) *Basis of Pay.*

(i) The rates of pay are fixed on a yearly or weekly basis, as described in sub-para. (C) below, and include pay for the whole period of a year or week, as the case may be.

(ii) The receipt of pay by an Official or Member as such, does not affect the payment of any Civil or War pension to which she may be entitled, or of any War Pension as the widow or dependant of an officer or soldier whose death was due to war service, or of any Navy and Army Separation Allowance of which she may be in receipt.

(B) *Gratuity for Members of the Mobile Branch.*

In addition to the revised rates of pay provided for by (C) below, a gratuity at the rate of 13s. a quarter, payable quarterly in arrear, will be granted to all Members of the Mobile Branch.

(C) *Rates of Pay.*

The following rates of pay for Members of the Mobile and Immobile Branches are applicable to all Stations at Home and Overseas:—

Learners' rate of pay in any Sub-category in which training is introduced will be 25s. per week except those whose pay is less than 25s., the period being limited to 4 weeks.

Category "A"—*Clerical Section.*

Sub-category 1. Superintending Forewoman Clerk (Record Offices only, 1 to 20 Clerks) ... ... 45s. per week.

„ 2. Forewoman Clerk (one to five) ... ... 37s 6d.–39s. 6d. per week.

„ 3. *Shorthand Typists (with a speed of 100 words a minute) ... ... 43s.–45s. per week.

„ 4. Ordinary General Clerks—
  (a) Suitable for Secretarial work but not necessarily shorthand typists, unless specified ... ...
  (b) Able to work without supervision, or able to supervise.
  (c) Copying, mostly to work under supervision ... ...
  (d) Typists ... ...
  (e) Register clerk for filing, card indexing, &c. ... ...
  (f) Book-keeping ...
  (g) Ledger keeping
  (h) Account keeping ...
  (j) Pay sheets ... ...
  (k) Returns ... ...
  (l) Accountants... ...
  (m) Librarians ... ...
  (n) Telephone clerks ...

27s. 6d.–33s. 6d. per week.

* Members now serving will retain their existing rates unless they pass a test giving a speed of over 100 words a minute. Should a shorthand typist be exceptionally employed in future with a speed of less than 100 words, the rate of pay will be 37s. 6d. These may be promoted Forewoman Clerks retaining their pay as Shorthand Typists.

Category "B"—*Household Section.*

Sub-category 1. Forewoman for Hostel
," 2. Forewoman Cook for—
    (a) Officers' Messes
    (b) Officers' Cadet Battalion of over 100 Cadets (one to each kitchen)
    (c) Men's Cookhouses (one to each cookhouse)

> Mobile £45 per annum. Immobile (enrolled before 1st February, 1918) 31s. 6d. per week.

," 3. Forewoman Waitress for—
    (a) Officers' Messes
    (b) Officers' Cadet Battalion of over 100 Cadets
," 4. Forewoman Laundress

> Mobile £40 per annum. Immobile (enrolled before 1st February, 1918.) 29s. 6d. per week.

," 5. Assistant Forewoman for Serjeants' Mess
    (a) Cook
    (b) Waitress
," 6. Laundresses—
    (a) Assistant Forewoman Laundress
    (b) Laundress
," 7. Cooks for—
    (a) Officers' Mess
    (b) Officers' Cadet Battalion
    (c) Serjeants' Mess
    (d) Hostel
    (e) Men's Cookhouses
," 8. Waitresses for—
    (a) Officers' Mess
    (b) Officers' Cadet Battalion
," 9. Pantrymaids for—
    (a) Serjeants' Mess
    (b) Men's Dining Rooms
," 10. Housemaids for all Units
," 11. Vegetable women, for all Units
," 12. By-product women, for all Units

> Mobile £26 per annum. Immobile (enrolled before 1st February, 1918) 24s. per week.

," 13. General Domestic Workers, for all Units

> Mobile £24 to £25 per annum. Immobile (enrolled before 1st February, 1918) 23s. to 23s. 6d. per week.

35

Category "C"—*Mechanical Section for Service Overseas only.*

Sub-category 1. Forewoman (Qualified Driver Mechanic) ... ... 40s. per week.
" 2.‡Qualified Driver Mechanics—
    (a) Ford ... ...
    (b) Other makes; all drivers should have had at least 3 months' driving, and should be able to undertake greasing, oiling, minor repairs and tyre changing ...
    (c) Tender drivers ...
    (d) Drivers of large cars not fitted with dual ignition ... ...
} 35s. per week.

Category "D"—*General Unskilled (Miscellaneous Section).*

Sub-category 1. Forewoman, unskilled ... 28s.–30s. per week.
    Assistant Forewoman, unskilled 26s.–28s. "
" 2.—(a) Storehousewomen ...
    (b) Packers ... ...
    (c) Issuers ... ...
    (d) Messengers ... ...
    (e) Checkers ... ...
    (f) Leading Hands ...
    (g) General unskilled labour ... ...
    (h) Sausage Makers ...
    (j) Chaff Cutters ...
} 24s.–26s. per week.

Category "E"—*Telephone and Postal Services for Overseas only (Clerical Section).*

Sub-category 1. Forewoman Telephonist ... 40s. per week.
" 2. " Telegraphist ... 50s. "
" 3. " Sorter ... ... 35s. "
" 4. Telephonists ... ... 35s. "
" 5. Telegraphists ... ... 42s. "
" 6. Sorters ... ... 30s. "
" 7. Postwomen ... ... 24s.–26s. per week.

‡ Will not be sent Overseas without a proficiency card or certificate.

Category " F "—*Miscellaneous* (*Miscellaneous Section*).

Sub-category 1. (a) Forewoman Printer ⎫ 42/- p w.
     (b)   "   Gardener ⎪
     (c)   "   Groom ⎬ 30s. per week.
     (d)   "   Shoemaker ⎪
     (e)   "   Baker ⎪
     (f)   "   Tailor ⎭

"   2. (a) Printers' Warehouse-⎫ 35/- to 36/- p 0
     women, binders and ⎪
     folders ⎬ 25s.–29s. per week.
    (b) Shoemakers ⎪
    (c) Bakers ⎭

"   3. Tailors   25s.–28s. per week.

"   4. (a) Gardeners ⎫ 26s. per week.
"   (b) Grooms (Women riders) ⎭

Category " G "—*Technical Employment* (*Mechanical Section*).

Sub-category 1. Forewoman (Technical)   38s.–42s. per week.

"   2. Assistant Forewoman
    (Technical)   32s.–36s. per week.

"   3. (a) Acetylene Welders ⎫
     must be fully trained ⎪
     in all descriptions of ⎪
     acetylene welding ⎪
    (b) Electricians for elec- ⎪
     tric depositing work; ⎪
     need not have electri- ⎪
     cal experience, but ⎪
     must be able to work ⎪
     neatly ⎪
    (c) Magneto Repairers, ⎬ 28s.–32s.
     vide Instrument Re- ⎪ per week.
     pairers ⎪
    (d) Fitters for viewing ⎪
    (e) Fitters for scraping and ⎪
     running in new bear- ⎪
     ings ⎪
    (f) Engine fitters for valve ⎪
     grinding, cylinder and ⎪
     piston ring lapping, ⎪
     stripping and cylinder ⎪
     cleaning ⎪
    (g) General Fitters, must ⎪
     be able to use file ⎪
     hammer, chisel, &c. ⎭

Category "G"—*Technical Employment (Mechanical Section)—continued.*

Sub-category 3—*continued.*

Machinists for the following machines:—
- (h) Capstan Lathes ...
- (j) Milling Machines ...
- (k) Drilling ,, ...
- (l) Slotting ,, ...
- (m) Grinding ... ...

There is practically no repetition work, it is therefore necessary that Capstan and other hands should be competent to do at least 6 operations ...

- (n) Turners, who must be capable of doing all descriptions of Plain turning ... ...
- (o) Instrument repairers, must at least know how to use watchmakers' and fine tools
- (p) Tinsmiths, must have had previous experience of tinsmiths' work ... ...
- (q) Coppersmiths, must have had previous experience ... ...
- (r) Armature Winders, must have had training ... ...
- (s) Vulcanisers, should produce Harvey Frost certificate of proficiency ... ...
- (t) Sand Blasters ...
- (u) Sheet Metal Workers
- (v) Wireless Mechanics ...
- (w) Aeroplane riggers ...
- (x) Cycle Fitter ... ...

28s. – 32s. per week.

Sub-category 4.
- (a) Forewoman (Unskilled) 32s.–34s. per week.
- (b) Assistant Forewomen (Unskilled) ... ... 28s.–30s. per week.

Category "G"—*Technical Employment (Mechanical Section)—continued.*

Sub-category 4—*continued.*

  (c) Dopers
  (d) Painters, with knowledge of plain painting
  (e) Sign writers
  (f) Carpenters
    } 25s.–30s. per week.

" 5. (a) Forewoman Storekeepers (Technical)   38s.–42s. per week.

  (b) Assistant Forewomen Storekeepers (Technical)   32s.–36s. per week.

  (c) Storekeepers for technical stores, with knowledge of engine parts and tools.

  (d) Storekeepers for Army Service Corps and Motor Transport, with knowledge of names of motor and engine parts, acquainted with names of usual electricians' and engineers' tools, must write well.
    } 28s.–32s. per week.

" 6. (a) Forewoman Storekeeper (Unskilled)   32s.–34s. per week.

  (b) Assistant Forewomen Storekeepers (Unskilled)   28s.–30s. per week.

  (c) Storekeepers, without technical knowledge, who only handle stores   24s.–26s. per week.

  Note.— Storekeepers, 5 (c) and 5 (d), will be employed to replace qualified soldier storemen only. Where replacement of ordinary labour in connection with storekeeping is required, storekeepers, 6 (c), will be employed.

" 7. (a) Forewoman Fabric Workers (Unskilled)   32s.–34s. per week.

Category "G"—*Technical Employment (Mechanical Section)*—continued.

Sub-category 7—*continued*.

    (b) Assistant Forewomen Fabric Workers (Unskilled) ... ... 28s.–30s. per week.

    (c) Sailmakers
    (d) Fabric Workers
    (e) Wing Workers
    (f) Canvas Stitchers
    (g) Upholsterers
    (h) Body Trimmers
    (j) Basket Makers
    (k) Tent Makers
    (l) Leather Stitchers

    All required mostly for heavy stitching.   25s.–29s. per week.

   8. (a) Forewoman Tracers and Colourists (Technical) ... 38s.–42s. per week.

    (b) Assistant Forewomen Tracers and Colourists (Technical) ... 32s.–36s. per week.

    (c) Tracers, highly skilled
    (d) Colourists ... ...   30s.–35s. per week.

   9. (a) Photographers ... 30s. per week.†

(D) *Transfers and Authority for Fixing Rates of Pay.*

Initial Rate of Pay.

(i) All Workers will be enrolled at the minimum rate of their sub-category. If a Worker is found to have any very special qualifications, she may be advanced to a higher rate of pay immediately after enrolment, if recommended in writing by the Selection Board, on joining the Receiving Depôt.

Subsequent Increases.

(ii) After she joins her unit, if a Worker is found to have very special qualifications, she may be immediately advanced by the O.C. to a higher rate within the range of the sub-category. These cases, again, should be quite exceptional. In other cases Workers, if thoroughly proficient in their work, may be advanced by the O.C. to a higher rate of pay within

---

† Rising at the discretion of the O.C. by increments of 2s. at intervals of not less than 2 months to 40s. The rate of 40s. will only be paid to fully skilled photographers (when qualified to replace a 1st class air mechanic).

the range of the sub-category, but such increases will not be granted more frequently than once a month, and no monthly increase will exceed one shilling in the weekly wage.

Transfers to a Higher Paid Sub-category.

(iii) Transfers to a higher paid sub-category may be authorized by the O.C. provided that the Member is thoroughly efficient in her new occupation, when she will commence work at the minimum rate of pay of the new range. Such transfers do not include promotion to Forewoman (*see* para. 12).

Voluntary Transfers from one Category to another.

(iv) Voluntary transfers from one category to another, and the Member's subsequent employment within the new category, may be authorized by the O.C. provided that the Member is thoroughly efficient in her new occupation. In such cases she will commence work at the minimum rate in the new range.

Transfers for Inefficiency.

(v) Where a Member is found to be inefficient at the work at which she is employed, a transfer may be authorized in the public interest by the O.C. from one category to another, or from one sub-category to another, even though such transfer may involve a reduction in the rate of pay. This procedure is not permissible as a disciplinary measure. A Member's rate of pay, however, within the range of any specific sub-category may not be reduced for any reason within that sub-category. Before such action is taken careful consideration will be given as to the advisability of giving the Member a further trial in another unit.

Transfers on Medical Grounds.

(vi) When a Member is medically unfit for her work she may be transferred, subject to para. (iv) above, to another category or sub-category, by the O.C. on the recommendation of a Medical Officer.

Medical Certificates.

(vii) In all cases when a Member is transferred by the O.C. to a category, or sub-category, involving greater physical strain, a Medical Certificate will be sent to the Officer i/c Q.M. A.A.C. Records, stating that she is fit to perform her work in her new category or sub-category.

(E) *Issue of Pay.*

Officials at Home.

(i) Officials at Home will draw their pay monthly in arrear, as from the date of taking up duty.

Members.

(ii) The pay of a Member will be issued from the agreed date of joining. If she is not called up on that date, but joins immediately on receiving A.F. W. 3630 at a later date, she will be entitled to pay from the agreed date of joining. The agreed date will be inserted by the Selection Board, or, in the case of Immobile Members, by the O.C., in para. 16 of the Enrolment Form (*see* Appendix A). In the event of not receiving a calling-up notice the Member will report, week by week, either personally or in writing to the nearest local Labour Exchange Official.

(F) *Advance of Pay.*

When a Member is about to proceed Overseas, an advance of pay not exceeding £1, in addition to pay due for service prior to embarkation, may be made by the Official of the Depôt concerned.

(G) *Deductions from Pay.*

Deductions from pay, for absence without leave, or in excess of paid leave, will be made at the rate of one day's pay for each day or part of a day's absence. A day's absence will be reckoned the same as for Soldiers under Section 138 (note 3) and Section 140 (2) of the Army Act.

(H) *Additional Categories.*

(i) When employments exist, not explicitly provided for by para. 21 (C), it will be found that in most cases they already fall within one of the prescribed headings, and can be classified to correspond with one of the categories provided for.

When new categories or sub-categories and new rates of pay are required, application will be made to the War Office.

(J) *Method of Accounting.*

(i) For the purposes of pay, &c., Members, other than those in Receiving Depôts, will be attached to convenient units, formations or offices, and administered accordingly.

(ii) Receiving Depôts, however, will form separate accounting units.

(iii) Detailed instructions *re* method of accounting are shown in Appendix E.

22. *ACCOMMODATION.*

(A) *Works Services.*

Any Works Services required should be requisitioned in writing on the local Commanding Royal Engineers or his accredited Representative as laid down in Para. 266, Regulations for Engineer Services (Part I).

(B) Officials and Members, other than those Officials whose enrolment does not include free quarters, will be accommodated as follows:—

Mobile Branch.—(i) In Quarters.
               (ii) In Approved Lodgings.
               (iii) In their own homes, provided there is no loss of efficiency in their work by so doing.

Immobile Branch.—In their own homes (*see* para. 1 (B)).

(C) *Receiving Depôts and Quarters.*

(i) *Receiving Depôts.*

All Receiving Depôts are administered direct from the War Office except as regards discipline and local administration which will be undertaken by Headquarters of Commands in which the depôts are situated. Applications for permanent staff for Receiving Depôts will be made to the War Office.

(ii) *Receiving Depôts for Service at Home.*

Receiving Depôts are established at certain centres for the purpose of collecting and despatching Members of the Mobile Branch to the units, formations or offices to which they will subsequently be attached for work, and providing them with uniform.

(iii) *Receiving Depôts for Overseas.*

(*a*) A Special Receiving Depôt has been established for the preparation of Overseas drafts.

(*b*) Suitable Officials and Members for service Overseas will be selected and sent in due course to this Depôt, where they will be provided with uniform, and be inoculated and vaccinated.

(iv) *Quarters.*

(*a*) Quarters will be established for the housing of Officials entitled to free quarters and Members of the Mobile Branch in close proximity to the unit, formation or office to which they are attached for work.

(*b*) Quarters may be conveniently divided into four types, which may be utilized in the order named:—

    (i) Existing Government quarters not requiring structural alterations.
    (ii) A suitable building or buildings loaned for the purpose.

(iii) Existing Government quarters or hutments only requiring minor adaptation.
(iv) A hired building or group of buildings.

(c) Proposals at Home under (b) (i) and (iii) will in every case be submitted for War Office sanction, with a statement showing the original purpose for which the quarters and hutments were provided, on which grounds they can now be misappropriated for the use of the Q.M.A.A.C., and whether such misappropriation if approved is likely to lead to a later request for the provision of any new buildings or huts in lieu of those proposed for use of the Q.M.A.A.C.; also the cost involved in adapting the buildings or hutments and the additional prospective cost, if any, when future reversion to original use is carried out.

(d) For establishments for Quarters, see Appendix B; and for scale of equipment, see Appendix C.

(D) *Washing Household Linen.*

The household linen of the Depôts or Quarters will be washed at the public expense in addition to the articles referred to in para. 23 (c). Care will be taken that due economy is exercised in the washing of household linen, and in no case will the following maximum scale be exceeded, except at Receiving Depôts, when the scale will vary according to the numbers passing through.

(i) Blankets ... ... To be exchanged as laid down for troops in para. 616, Regulations for Supply, Transport and Barrack Services.

(ii) Cases, slip, pillow: sheets; and towels (Turkish). } 1 per week per head for Officials and Members.

(iii) Cloths, glass
(iv) Dusters
(v) Towels, hand
(vi) Towels, round
} 50 per cent. of the quantity in the Schedules (*see* Appendix C) to be washed once a week.

(E) *Contingent Allowance.*

(i) Contingent allowance will be granted to Q.M.A.A.C. Headquarters, Receiving Depôts and Quarters, to cover expenses properly chargeable to Army funds, such as small repairs and cleaning material, in cases where it is not practicable to arrange for the work to be done or materials supplied from the normal Army services.

(ii) The yearly rates are as follows:—
Not less than 20 Members, £2; for every additional completed ten Members, £1.

(iii) The allowance will be calculated on the average number present during the month preceding the date on which the claim is made.

(iv) Where, in exceptional cases, the numbers in Quarters are temporarily less than 20, a proportionately reduced allowance may be issued.

(F) *Barrack Damages, etc.*

(i) (a) Officials in charge of Depôts and Quarters will be held responsible for the custody of the furniture, stores, clothing stores, &c., committed to their keeping.

(ii) No collective or individual stoppages for barrack damages can be enforced against Members, but when any Member wilfully or negligently damages Government property or otherwise wilfully or negligently causes damage in breach of her contract of service, fines may be enforced against individual Members in accordance with paras. 14 and 15 of Army Form W. 3578, Enrolment Form (*see* Appendix A).

(G) *Approved Lodgings at Home.*

(i) The following " Q.M.A.A.C. Approved Lodging Scheme " is in lieu of billeting under the provisions of " The Billeting of Civilians Act." It is intended to provide solely for parties in cases where it is impossible to obtain other quarters, or when Immobile Members are not employed.

(ii) It is not intended that it should be used to accommodate Members during the time Quarters are being prepared, and it will only be applicable to the Mobile Branch.

(iii) This scheme will not be used without War Office Authority.

(iv) In forwarding A.F. W. 3631 to the War Office, Commands will report the circumstances which make it impossible to obtain other quarters, and attach an application for permission to use this scheme.

(v) If sanction is given, Commands will instruct the O.C. the unit, requiring the women to request the nearest Employment Exchange to select suitable lodgings, and arrange for them to be approved by the Q.M.A.A.C. Commands will issue orders for the inspection of, and report on, the approved lodgings.

When the Q.M.A.A.C. Official has approved the lodgings she will notify the Command through the Q.M.A.A.C. Controller of:—

    (i) The address of the lodgings.
    (ii) The number each house can accommodate, and
    (iii) The date on which the lodgings can be taken up.
    (iv) Whether central messing and washing arrangements can be made.

The Controller will also convey this information to the Receiving Depôts in the Command.

Requisitions for women who are intended to be accommodated in approved lodgings will be met in the usual manner from Receiving Depôts.

(vi) The price of the lodgings will be arranged with the landlady by the Employment Exchange, who will notify the Official, to whose Unit the Member is attached, who will take the necessary action.

(vii) The Employment Exchange will arrange for the price of the lodgings:—

(a) Lodging and service.
(b) Board.
(c) Washing,

and the lodgings will, or will not, include (b) and (c), according to whether the member's food and washing will be provided by the landlady or not.

(viii) 14s. per week will be deducted from the lodged Member's pay (with the exception of Mobile Members shown in paragraph 21 (C) Category "B"), in the same way as if she was living in Quarters.

(ix) Any balance due to the landlady will be borne by the State, and the O.C. concerned will be responsible for payment for the lodgings.

(x) Lodgings will not be more than one mile from the Member's work, and arrangements will be made for central messing and personal washing under Army arrangements for lodged Members.

(xi) In cases where these arrangements cannot be carried out War Office approval must be secured.

(H) *Hutments.*

In cases where accommodation consists of Hutments which are not provided with bunks, an acting Assistant Forewoman will be placed in charge of each hut (*see* para. 4 B (ii)).

(J) *Arrangements for Officials and Members in Summer Camps.*

(a) When units, to whom personnel of the Q.M.A.A.C. are attached, go under canvas, every endeavour will be made to procure suitable buildings in the neighbourhood.

(b) Where this is found to be entirely impossible, the women must be placed under canvas in carefully chosen and prepared camps, which must be properly isolated, screened and protected from the rest of the camp, and ablution and latrine accommodation provided as in standing camps. The Official concerned will always be consulted.

(c) For the scale of camp equipment for Officials and Members when accommodated under canvas, *see* Appendix Z<small>A</small>.

This equipment will be additional to that authorized for the military formation to which the Officials and Members are attached.

23. BOARD, LODGING, SERVICE* AND WASHING.

(a) Officials and Members living in their own homes will find their own board, lodging, service and washing, and no deductions will therefore be made in this respect.

(b) A deduction at a fixed rate per week will be made from the pay of all Officials and Members at Home and Overseas accommodated under War Department arrangements other than those whose emoluments include free board, lodging and washing. The rates at present approved are:—Officials, 15s. 6d. per week; Members, 14s. per week.

(c) These sums will cover the provision by the War Department of board, lodging, service, and, in the case of Members, free washing of eight pieces of personal clothing, and as many handkerchiefs as required, per week, in addition to caps, aprons, overalls, &c., used on the public service and washed at the public expense. Officials will make their own arrangements for their washing without expense to the Public.

(d) In cases where collective arrangements cannot be made conveniently for washing, the deduction from pay for board, lodging, and service will be at the weekly rate of 12s. 6d. for Members; in which event they will make arrangements for their own washing.

(e) All Members in Category "B" employed in the Mobile Branch are entitled to free board, lodging, service and washing. 1s. 6d. a week to meet laundry expenses on personal clothing will be allowed when arrangements for washing at the public expense cannot be made.

24. FUEL AND LIGHT ALLOWANCES.

The scale of allowance for fuel for all purposes in Quarters for all grades will be at the rates laid down in Allowance Regulations, paras. 196, 197, 198 and 202. Light will be admissible in respect of authorized burners.

25. RATIONS AT HOME AND OVERSEAS.

(a) Scales of rations for Home and Overseas as laid down in Appendix D, which may be amended from time to time, will be issuable in accordance with the Allowance Regulations to the Official in charge of Quarters in respect of all Officials and Members accommodated therein.

---

* Service includes the provision of fuel, light, water and cleaning materials.

(b) The Official concerned or, if the Members are attached for rations to an Army Unit, the O.C., will be responsible for the feeding arrangements within the limits of this provision. The rations and the commuted allowance will be accounted for in the usual Army manner (*see* Appendix E), and the administration of the commuted allowance will follow the usual Army rules.

26. RATION AND LODGING ALLOWANCE.

(a) In the case of Officials who are entitled to free quarters, and are not able to obtain accommodation in War Department Depôts or Quarters, a lodging allowance of 2s. 3d a day will be given in lieu (in the case of the Chief Controller in France, 3s. a day).

(b) Members of Category "B" (Mobile Branch) (*see* para 21 (C)) when on paid ordinary leave will receive 2s. a day "Ration and Lodging Allowance." Members enrolled before the date of these Regulations when on sick leave will draw 1s. 6d. a day for rations and 9d. a day for lodging allowance. Those enrolled after the date of these Regulations will receive consolidated allowance of 2s.

27. DEDUCTIONS DURING LEAVE.

When a Member is absent from her Quarters or Approved Lodging, or on leave (including sick leave), no deduction for board and lodging from her pay will be made for the days of her absence, and no rations or commuted allowance under para. 25 (a) and (b) will be drawn.

28. REGIMENTAL INSTITUTES.

Use of Regimental Institutes, with the exception of the wet bar, is permitted to Officials and Members, exclusively for one half-hour daily out of the time during which it is usually open.

Application for the use of the Institute will be made to the O.C. concerned by the local Official. The O.C. will make necessary arrangements.

29. SPIRITUAL MINISTRATION.

(a) Chaplains to the Forces and officiating clergymen appointed for duty with the troops should include in their ministrations such Officials or Members at their stations as are required to wear uniform. (*See* para. 19.)

(b) Remuneration for the extra work involved will, in the case of officiating clergymen, be made by including the number of such personnel in computing the amounts payable under A.O. 12 of 1916.

30. FUNERALS.

Officials and Members who die while serving may be granted the honours of a Military funeral, but without a firing party. The burial will, in the case of an Official or Member dying while serving with an Expeditionary Force, be carried out by the Military Authorities, and the cost borne by the public. If in any case the friends or relatives are allowed to make the arrangements the whole cost will be borne by them.

In the case of an Official or Member dying while serving in the United Kingdom, free conveyance by rail of the body from the station to the home in the United Kingdom will be allowed, provided that the relatives express a desire that the body should be sent home, and are not in a position to bear the cost themselves. A.F. W. 3084, which can be obtained from the nearest military hospital, will in such cases be used.

31. WOMEN'S LEGION.

(A) *Motor Transport Section.*

Accommodation in Q.M.A.A.C. Quarters may be provided for Motor Drivers of the Women's Legion. Officials of the Q.M.A.A.C. are in no way concerned in the control and discipline of the Women's Legion.

(B) *Military Cookery Section.*

(i) Members of this section who are unable to enrol in the Q.M.A.A.C. will be permitted to complete their present contracts. On termination of their contracts they will have the alternative of joining the Q.M.A.A.C., or of being discharged, when they will be replaced by Workers of the Q.M.A.A.C. Whilst completing their present contracts, they will be administered by the A.G.'s Department of the War Office on identical lines with the Q.M.A.A.C., and will be subject to the control of its Officials.

(ii) Any Members who are unable on the expiration of their contract to enrol in the Q.M.A.A.C. should apply to:—

    The General Secretary,
        Headquarters, Women's Legion,
            115, Victoria Street, London, S.W.

and every effort will be made to find them suitable civilian employment outside the Army.

32. RE-ENROLMENT OF CERTAIN EXISTING PERSONNEL OF THE Q.M.A.A.C. INTO THE MOBILE BRANCH ONLY.

(a) A Member who enrolled prior to 7th July, 1917, may, without further medical examination, be re-enrolled by her

O.C., who will complete and obtain the Member's signature to Army Form W. 3578 (*see* Appendix A), and himself sign the form, as Approving Officer, and Army Form W. 3577, as Approving Military Authority. Her number will be the same as that given to her on original enrolment. The O.C. will subsequently forward both these Army Forms, together with a Nominal Roll showing the Unit, Station, nature of Employment, and Rate of Pay allotted to each Member, and quoting her official number, to the Officer i/c Q.M.A.A.C. Records, at Home or Overseas.

Such Members will no longer be eligible to receive the £5 Bonus to which they were entitled under their previous engagement, but they will receive the proportion due to them up to the date of re-enrolment and become eligible for the Gratuity under para 21 (B) above, and also to the higher rates of pay laid down in para. 21 (C).

PART II.

RECRUITING.

GENERAL INSTRUCTIONS.

33. *PROVISION OF WOMEN.*

The provision of Members for the Q.M.A.A.C. will be carried out by the Adjutant-General's Department of the War Office in conjunction with the Employment Department of the Ministry of Labour.

34. *RESERVED OCCUPATIONS.*

(A) *Debarred from Enrolment.*

Existing employees and those employed subsequently in any of the following departments are debarred from enrolment into either the Mobile or Immobile Branches unless they produce a letter from their employer or head of department, stating that they have permission to apply for enrolment:—

- (i) All Government Departments (including the War Office and Military Pay Offices at Home, but excluding all other Military Offices).
- (ii) Establishments (other than Military Units) under the control of the War Office.
- (iii) Forces of the Overseas Dominions (except as agreed with their respective Headquarters).

(iv) Munition Factories.
(v) Controlled Firms.
(vi) Voluntary Aid Detachments. Military Hospitals or Red Cross Hospitals.
(vii) Schools (Teachers).
(viii) Municipal Enterprises.
(ix) Firms engaged on Government Contracts.
(x) Agriculture.

(B) *Temporarily Debarred from Enrolment.*

No action will be taken at present regarding enrolment into either the Mobile or Immobile Branches of women employed at Home by:—

(i) Army Ordnance Department.
(ii) Navy and Army Canteen Board.
(iii) Administrative Member of the Forage Committee.

35 *ALIENS.*

(a) Only British subjects (including naturalized British subjects) will be enrolled.
(b) Subject to the above no woman, either of whose parents or whose husband is or has been at any time of alien nationality, may be summoned before a Selection Board or be enrolled until either M. 40/9 (Appendix K), or M. 40/9A (Appendix L), and M. 40/11 (Appendix N) have been submitted to and approved by the War Office.

36. *ADVERTISEMENTS.*

Advertisements, notices, posters, or publicity in any form, asking for recruits will be arranged for by the Ministry of Labour, or, in special cases, by the War Office.

37. *ENROLMENT FORM.*

The attention of those responsible for the enrolment of women is drawn to the following alterations which will be made pending reprinting to existing Enrolment Forms, as shown in Appendix A:—

(a) Paragraph 11, the words " Sub-category " to be inserted in two places.
(b) The foot note to paragraph 11 to be altered from " Section," " Category " to " Category," " Sub-Category."
(c) One month's notice of termination of service will be substituted for the notice of one week in the case of the Mobile Branch only (*see* paragraph 16 of

A.F. W. 3578). One week's notice will remain in force for the Immobile Branch.
(d) In the Woman's declaration the words " Army Council Instructions " will be altered to "the Regulations for the Q.M.A.A.C."

38. ENROLMENT.

(a) Enrolment will be either into the Mobile Branch, paragraph 1 (A), or the Immobile Branch, paragraph 1 (B).
(b) No women will be enrolled for Category B (para. 21 (C)) for the Immobile Branch.
(c) The minimum age for service at Home will be 18 years, Overseas 20 years.
(d) No Official or Member whose husband is serving Overseas in the same theatre of War will be eligible for employment Overseas. If the husband is subsequently ordered to the same theatre of war, the Official or Member will be withdrawn and employed at Home.
(The question of enrolling girls under 18 is being considered.)

39. SPECIAL INSTRUCTIONS FOR ENROLMENT INTO THE MOBILE BRANCH.

(A) *Enrolment for.*

The enrolment of women for the Mobile Branch (para. 1 (A)) will be carried out by Selection and Medical Boards at various centres throughout the country.

(B) *Assistant Chief Controller i/c Personnel and Recruiting Controllers.*

The Assistant Chief Controller i/c Personnel is attached to Headquarters, Q.M.A.A.C.; Recruiting Controllers are allotted to Headquarters of certain Areas.

(C) *Method of Indenting* :—
  (i) G.Os.C.-in-C. will submit returns to the War Office monthly on A.F. W. 3631 (*see* Appendix F) of Members required. The prospective occupations of all such Members will be described in accordance with para. 21 (C).
  (ii) In the case of technical Members required in formations administered direct from the War Office the return will be forwarded to the War Office through Command Headquarters in which the Unit is stationed.
  (iii) Members required to replace casualties will be indented for in a similar manner as required.

(D) *Duties of a Recruiting Controller.*

The duties of a Recruiting Controller will be as follows:—

(i) She will work under the orders of the Controller of Personnel, in close conjunction with the Divisional Officers of the Ministry of Labour.

(ii) She will correspond officially with the Officials mentioned in (D) (i).

(iii) On receipt of demands from the Assistant Chief Controller i/c Personnel she will place herself in communication with the Divisional Officers of the Ministry of Labour, and will, in conjunction with them, arrange for Selection and Medical Boards.

(iv) When Boards are held at the Receiving Depôt she will be responsible for seeing that the accommodation and medical appliances (*see* Appendix C, Schedules 19, 20 and 21) which are provided in the Depôt are in order. When Boards are held at other centres she will arrange with the Employment Exchange for the provision of accommodation and such medical appliances as are not portable.

(v) She will be President of all Selection Boards held in her area, and will arrange for a local Official of the Q.M.A.A.C., and a representative of the Employment Department, Ministry of Labour, to act as members. She will also authorize additional panels whenever necessary. When technical women are being selected she will apply to the Assistant Chief Controller i/c Personnel, with a view to obtaining the services of a technical Army Officer in an advisory capacity.

(vi) She will notify the President of the Medical Board (para. 49) of the date, place and time of the proposed Selection Board.

(vii) She will be responsible for the enrolment of selected women and will act as Approving Officer as defined in A.F. W. 3578 (Appendix A) and will insert in para. 16 the date on which the Member agrees to join for duty. She will hand to each Member, after she has been enrolled, " Acknowledgment of Enrolment " Form, M.40/13 (*see* Appendix G).

(viii) She will be responsible that the provisions of para. 8 regarding the disposal of the documents of selected women are complied with.

(ix) At the conclusion of each Selection Board she will be responsible that the Nominal Roll M.40/14 (*see* Appendix H) is completed in triplicate, handing two copies to the Divisional Officer of the Ministry of Labour and retaining one copy for her own use. In completing this form due regard will be paid to the

agreed date of joining and accommodation available at the Receiving Depôt. In the case of women selected locally for local employment, the Recruiting Controller will forward the Nominal Roll M40/14 of the women selected to the Official concerned, who will arrange with the Divisional Officer of the Ministry of Labour for the posting of women to their units.
(x) At the conclusion of each Selection Board she will forward a return, A.F. W. 3632, in accordance with Appendix J, to the Officer i/c Q.M.A.A.C. Records.

(E) *Ministry of Labour.*

The Divisional Officer of the Ministry of Labour will be responsible for:—

(i) The despatch of Application Form M.40/9 (*see* Appendix K) to applicants wishing to join the Q.M.A.A.C.
(ii) A postcard acknowledgement of the receipt of application M.40/10 (*see* Appendix M).
(iii) The despatch of Reference Forms M.40/11 (*see* Appendix N) to the persons indicated in the reply to Question 20 on the Form of Application M.40/9 (*see* Appendix K).
(iv) The production of Application Forms and Reference Forms at the Selection Boards.
(v) The despatch to candidates of a Form of Summons, A.F. W. 3629 (*see* Appendix O), together with the necessary railway warrant for each candidate required to attend before the Selection and Medical Boards.

Candidates will not be interviewed by Boards unless and until the necessary references have been taken up. The minimum number of references for this purpose will be two, one must be from her recent or present employer.
(vi) The despatch of A.F W. 3630 (Appendix P) calling up selected Members to the address specified on M.40/14 (Appendix H), including provision of the necessary train arrangements and supervision of their entrainment.
(vii) The completion and despatch of M.40/14 (Appendix H) in due course.
(viii) All correspondence regarding delays, &c., in calling up Members will be carried out direct between the responsible officer of the Ministry of Labour and the Official of the Receiving Depôt or the O.C. the unit concerned.

(F) *Medical Boards.*
See para. 49.

(G) *Travelling Expenses prior to Enrolment, on Joining and on Termination of Engagement.*
See para. 18 (E).

40. *SPECIAL INSTRUCTIONS FOR ENROLMENT OF WOMEN, EXCEPT THOSE ALREADY EMPLOYED WITH THE ARMY, INTO THE IMMOBILE BRANCH.*

The enrolment will be carried out as follows:—

(a) The O.C. will endeavour in the first instance to obtain the number of women authorized through the local Employment Exchange Official, and will at the same time inform him whether the women are entitled to uniform in accordance with para. 19 (A).

(b) The Employment Exchange Officer will be responsible for informing the women before enrolment whether they are entitled to wear uniform.

(c) The prospective occupations of the women will be described in accordance with para. 21 (C).

(d) The Employment Exchange Officer will issue a Form of Application M.40/9A (*see* Appendix L), and will obtain at least two replies from referees for each applicant M.40/11 (*see* Appendix N), also a Medical Certificate in accordance with Appendix S.

(e) The completed references, if considered satisfactory by the Employment Exchange Officer, together with the Medical Certificate, will be forwarded to the O.C., who may thereupon complete and obtain the woman's signature to A.F. W. 3578 (Appendix A), and himself enrol the woman and sign A.F. W. 3578 as Approving Officer, and insert in para. 16 the date the Member agrees to join for duty. He will also sign A.F. W. 3577 as Approving Military Authority. A.F. W. 3578 will be endorsed on the front page with the word "Immobile," and the answer to para. 10 thereon will be "No, only at.............. (place)."

(f) The O.C. will subsequently forward both these Army Forms, together with completed references, Medical Certificate, and a Nominal Roll showing the unit, station, nature of employment, and rate of pay allotted to each Member to the Officer i/c Q.M.A.A.C. Records.

(g) The Nominal Roll will subsequently be returned to the unit by the Officer i/c Q.M.A.A.C. Records, with the Corps number allotted to each Member inserted thereon, and he will at the same time prepare and transmit to the O.C. A.F. B. 103 and A.F. B. 178 for each Member enrolled.

(h) The particulars given in the Identification Certificate will replace Table 1 of A.F. B. 178.

(j) If there is no Employment Exchange within five miles of the unit, or if the Employment Exchange Officer is unable to give the O.C. an assurance within three days of the demand that the requisite number of women will be available in a fortnight, the O.C. is at liberty to enrol suitable women living at home obtained through other sources. It is very desirable that the O.C. and the Local Officer of the Employment Exchange should work in the closest co-operation to avoid overlapping. The O.C. will on no account issue posters or advertise in the Press.

(k) The procedure in the case of such direct enrolment will be similar to that laid down in (a) and (b) above, the O.C. for this purpose replacing the Local Officer of the Employment Exchange, except that he will forward the Application Forms to the Local Officer of the Employment Exchange who will at once proceed to obtain the necessary Medical Certificate and forward it, together with the Application Form, to the O.C. concerned within three days. No other Medical Certificate will be accepted.

(l) The O.C. concerned will obtain all the necessary Application and Reference Forms from the nearest Employment Exchange (on no account will application for these forms be made to the War Office).

(m) The cost of the Medical Certificates (2s. 6d. per woman), whether approved or rejected, will be borne by the Ministry of Labour. All matters arising in connection with the Medical Certificates must be referred to the Local Officer of the Employment Exchange.

(n) When it is evident that sufficient local women are not obtainable to meet his requirements, the O.C. will notify the Local Officer of the Employment Exchange before applying for Mobile Members to complete his indents.

41. *SPECIAL INSTRUCTIONS. ENROLMENT OF WOMEN ALREADY EMPLOYED WITH THE ARMY INTO EITHER THE MOBILE OR IMMOBILE BRANCH.*

(A) *Mobile Branch.*

The enrolment will be carried out as follows:—
- (i) The O.C. will ascertain from the Recruiting Controller the date and place of Selection and Medical Boards before which applicants for enrolment can appear.
- (ii) The O.C. will send the appropriate Application Form, in the first instance, to the Local Officer of the Employment Exchange, stating the date and

place of the Selection Board, which the candidate is to attend. The Local Officer of the Employment Exchange will then return the Application Form to the O.C. with the requisite railway warrant in accordance with para. 18 (E).

(iii) The O.C. will send the Application Form, together with a letter of recommendation from himself in lieu of references to the Recruiting Controller three clear days before the date of the Board before which the woman is to appear.

In the case of members of the Women's Legion, the letter of recommendation will be endorsed by the Official under whom she is working. The responsibility for selection or rejection will in all cases rest with the Selection Board.

(iv) The enrolment will subsequently be carried out in accordance with the instructions for enrolment in the Mobile Branch (*see* para. 39).

In the case of members of the Women's Legion, the Enrolment Form will be endorsed on the top of the front page in red ink with the words " Women's Legion from *..................... (date)."

(B) *Immobile Branch.*

The enrolment will be carried out as follows:—

(i) The O.C. will send the appropriate Application Form to the Local Officer of the Employment Exchange, who will thereupon arrange for the medical examination of the candidate, and return the Application Form and Medical Certificate to the O.C. within three days.

(ii) The O.C. may thereupon enrol the woman in accordance with the instructions laid down for enrolment in the Immobile Branch, the completed Medical Certificate replacing the Certificate on A.F. W. 3578 (Appendix A).

(iii) The Form of Enrolment will be endorsed on the front page with the word " Immobile," and the answer to para. 10 will be " No, only at.......................... (Place)."

(iv) The completed Medical Certificate of women rejected for the Immobile Branch on medical grounds will be forwarded by the O.C. to the Controller of Medical Services, Q.M.A.A.C., Adastral House, London, E.C.

---

* The original date the Member joined the Women's Legion.

PART III.

MEDICAL SERVICES.

42. ORGANIZATION.

(a) The Medical Services of the Q.M.A.A.C. are controlled by the Director-General, Army Medical Service, who is responsible for the Medical Services of the Corps.

(b) An Auxiliary Section has been formed in the R.A.M.C. for this purpose, and suitable Medical Women are selected for appointment.

(c) The conditions under which they wear uniform are the same as for the Q.M.A.A.C., and the uniform is similar, except that they wear the collar and hat badges of the R.A.M.C., and an inset on the shoulder strap of similar colour to the facings of the R.A.M.C. (dull cherry).

(d) They are entitled to the uniform grant under the conditions laid down in para. 19.

The following appointments are authorized:—

Appointment.	Employment.	Badge to be worn on shoulder strap.
Controller of Medical Services.	Attached to H.Q. D.G.A.M.S. War Office.	1 Fleur de Lys and 2 roses.
Controller of Medical Services Overseas.	Attached to G.H.Q. Overseas.	1 Fleur de Lys and 2 roses.
Assistant Medical Controller.	Attached to H.Q., of Commands and to certain Areas Overseas.	1 Fleur de Lys.
Recruiting Medical Controller.	Attached to certain Recruiting Areas.	1 Fleur de Lys.
Medical Official ...	Attached to Receiving Depôts for Overseas and under War Office sanction to Women's Hospitals where instituted, and to certain large camps and to certain bases Overseas.	3 roses.

43. CONTROLLERS OF MEDICAL SERVICES, Q.M.A.A.C. AT HOME AND OVERSEAS.

(a) *At Home.*

The Controller of Medical Services is attached to the Office of the D.G.A.M.S., to whom she is responsible, and under whom she will exercise control over the administration of the medical and sanitary services of the Q.M.A.A.C. at Home. She will from time to time visit such Units as may be required, and report to the D.G.A.M.S., in writing, any medical or sanitary defects or requirements she considers should be brought to notice.

(b) *Overseas.*

The Controller of Medical Services is attached to G.H.Q., and is stationed at such place as will be most convenient for the discharge of her duties. All medical questions affecting the Q.M.A.A.C. Overseas will be submitted to superior authority through her. She will, from time to time, visit such units as may be required, and will report, in writing, to the D.G.M.S. any medical or sanitary defects or requirements she considers necessary to bring to notice.

44. ASSISTANT MEDICAL CONTROLLERS AT HOME AND OVERSEAS.

(a) One Assistant Medical Controller is attached to each Command at Home, and one to each of the Northern and Southern L. of C. Areas, Overseas. She acts as Adviser to the Administrative Medical Officer on medical and sanitary services connected with the Q.M.A.A.C.

(b) She will as required visit (except in the case of the Recruiting Medical Boards and the Receiving Depôts situated in her area, for which the Recruiting Medical Controller is directly responsible to the Controller of Medical Services):—

  (i) All sites and buildings proposed for the accommodation of the Q.M.A.A.C.
  (ii) All workshops, stores, buildings, and premises where the Q.M.A.A.C. are employed.
  (iii) All hospitals and rest camps for the accommodation of the Q.M.A.A.C.
  (iv) Each Unit or Detachment of the Q.M.A.A.C.

(c) After each inspection, she will submit a report in writing, together with any recommendations she considers desirable, to the Administrative Medical Officer.

(d) She will submit a fortnightly report in writing to the Administrative Medical Officer on the general health of the Q.M.A.A.C.

45. RECRUITING MEDICAL CONTROLLERS.

They are in medical and sanitary charge of the Receiving Depôt of the Recruiting Area to which they are attached, and will be available for such medical duties connected therewith, including the giving of health lectures, as may be allotted to them. They will be directly responsible to the Controller of Medical Services for all Recruiting Medical Boards in the Area, and will act as Presidents of such Boards.

46. MEDICAL OFFICIALS.

(a) One will be attached to each Receiving Depôt for Overseas, to each Hospital for the Q.M.A.A.C. when such Hospitals are established, and to certain bases Overseas for service with the Q.M.A.A.C. as required.

(b) One may also be appointed in medical charge of camps or centres where over 1,000 Members are employed.

(c) Medical Officials will be directly responsible to the Area Medical Controllers.

47. RATES OF PAY.

(a) The following rates of pay are approved for the Medical Women, appointed for duty with the Medical Services, Q.M.A.A.C. at Home and Overseas.

At Home and Overseas.

(i) Controller of Medical Services. £700 per annum inclusive.

(ii) Assistant Medical Controller, Recruiting Medical Controller, Medical Official, or any other whole time services. 24s. per diem and rations on the scale laid down for the Q.M.A.A.C., or the allowance of 1s. 6d. per diem in lieu of rations.

At Home.

(iii) Medical Women acting as Members of Travelling Medical Boards (full-time temporary services). 24s. per diem and rations on the scale laid down for the Q.M.A.A.C., or the allowance of 1s. 6d. per diem in lieu of rations on the days on which travelling allowance is not claimed.

(iv) Medical Women giving part-time services (employed as members of Medical Boards). Rates applicable to men doctors similarly employed in examining male recruits.

(b) The Controller of Medical Services at Home will be paid under War Office arrangements.

(c) In the case of other Medical Women serving under (a) (i) or (ii) above pay and (where admissible) ration allowance will be issued by the Command Paymaster of the Command in which they are employed, and in the case of Medical Women serving Overseas, by the Command Paymaster, Base. Claims will be rendered on A.F. O. 1679, which will be signed in the case of a Controller by a Staff Officer of Command Headquarters, in other cases by a Controller or a Staff Officer of Command Headquarters, as may be convenient.

(d) Medical Women referred to in (a) (iii) above will render claims on A.F. O. 1679 to the Command Paymaster of the Command in which their Headquarters are situated. Those under (a) (iv) employed intermittently at Home in connection with the Q.M.A.A.C. Medical Boards, will render claims for payment for each day worked on A.F. O. 1679 to the Command Paymaster of the Command in which they are employed. In each case the claims will be countersigned by the President of the Board.

(e) No Medical Woman serving with the Q.M.A.A.C. at Home or Overseas is entitled to accommodation in W.D. Depôts or Quarters. If they are exceptionally so accommodated, the charges will be as follows:—

 3s. a day for lodging, and
 3s. a day for board and service.

Adjustment will be made by abatement from the pay claimed on A.F. O. 1679.

(f) Claims for ration allowance under (a) (ii) and (iii) above will be supported by certificates that Rations could not be supplied on the days for which the allowance is claimed.

(g) Sick leave will be governed by Articles 480 and 481 of the Pay Warrant.

48. *RATES OF PENSION OR GRATUITY OF MEDICAL WOMEN.*

(a) If a Medical Woman serving at Home has to relinquish her appointment owing to injury or disease specifically attributable to her employment, she will be eligible for an award under Scale III. of the Treasury Warrant framed under Section I. of the Superannuation Act, 1887, based on the following scale according to the degree of impairment of earning capacity:—

 (i) Totally destroyed, an annual allowance of fifteen-sixtieths pay and emoluments, in addition to one-sixtieth pay and emoluments for each year of service.

(ii) Materially impaired, a gratuity not exceeding one year's pay and emoluments, or £100, whichever is less.

(iii) Impaired, two-thirds annual pay and emoluments, or £100, whichever is less.

(iv) Slightly impaired, one-third annual pay and emoluments, or £100, whichever is less.

(b) If a Medical Woman serving Overseas has to relinquish her appointment on account of injury or illness specifically attributable to her employment, she will be entitled to a pension under Scheme (No. 4), framed under the Injuries in War (Compensation) Act, 1914 (Session 2), according to the degree of impairment of earning capacity, as follows:—

(i) Totally destroyed ... ... 20/60 pay and emoluments
(ii) Materially impaired ... 15/60 ,, ,, ,,
(iii) Impaired ... ... 10/60 ,, ,, ,,
(iv) Slightly impaired ... ... 5/60 ,, ,, ,,

49. *MEDICAL BOARDS.*

(a) Medical Examination by a Board of Medical Women will be required before enrolment into the Mobile Branch.

(b) A Medical Woman will be President of the Medical Boards held in conjunction with Selection Boards. She will arrange for the attendance of two or more Medical Women to act as members.

(c) She will be directly responsible in all matters concerning the Boards to the Controller of Medical Services at Home.

(d) She will place the Members who are passed as medically fit in three categories:—

(i) Fit for General Service. (At Home or Overseas).
(ii) Fit for Home Service only.
(iii) Fit for Service in Immobile Branch only.

Any woman placed in category (iii) who wishes to be employed with the Immobile Branch can be accepted without further medical examination.

(e) She will fill up for each Member so passed A.F's. W. 3661 and B. 178, and will forward them at the conclusion of the Board to the Officer i/c Q.M.A.A.C. Records.

(f) If other Medical Boards are required in addition to those held at the recruiting centres, travelling Medical Boards will be arranged by the Controller of Medical Services.

(g) For provision of stationery, furniture and medical appliances for Medical Boards, see Appendix C (Schedules 19, 20, 21 and para. 39 D (iv)). For clerical assistance for Medical Boards, see Appendix B (8).

50. TRAVELLING ALLOWANCE.

(*a*) Travelling Allowance when absent on duty from their Headquarters may be claimed by the Medical Women enumerated under para. 47 (*a*) (i), (ii) and (iii) at the rates for Classes 7-14 and under the conditions laid down in the Allowance Regulations the issue of Detention Allowance being subject to the terms of A.C.I. 1199 of 1916.

(*b*) The Medical Women enumerated under para. 47 (*a*) (iv) may, if their rates of pay include no provision for travelling, claim 1st class travelling expenses by rail for all journeys they are required to make of more than 10 miles from their Headquarters together with travelling allowance at the rates, and under the conditions referred to at (*a*). These claims must be certified by the Recruiting Medical Controller, and countersigned by the Controller of Medical Services.

51. ADMISSION TO HOSPITALS.

(A) For the general conditions under which Officials and Members may be admitted to Hospitals, *see* para. 59.

(B) When Officials and Members are admitted to Military Hospitals (or to Civil Hospitals under special arrangements made by the War Office under para. 59), the general procedure will be as follows:—

(i) On admission to hospital, Officials and Members will be dealt with as laid down for regular soldiers in " General Instructions (3) " issued with A.C.I. 500 of 1918, so far as those instructions are applicable, and subject to the modifications shown below.

(ii) Pay:—
 (*a*) Officials and Members admitted to Military Hospitals Overseas will remain on the strength of their Accounting Unit.
 (*b*) Officials and Members serving at Home will remain on the strength of their Accounting Unit.
 (*c*) Officials and Members admitted to Military Hospitals at Home on return from Overseas will be dealt with as follows:—
  On receipt of a notification from the War Office that an Official or Member is admitted to hospital the Officer i/c Q.M.A.A.C. Records will at once inform the Official concerned, Receiving Depôt, London, of the fact. She will then take the Official or Member on the strength of the Depôt from the date of her admission to Hospital at Home.

(iii) When an Official serving at Home becomes seriously ill and her address cannot be obtained from the patient, the Officer i/c Hospital will telegraph to the Officer i/c Q.M.A.A.C. Records, asking that a telegram may be sent direct to the next-of-kin.

(iv) Except in the case of patients who are likely to be unfit for further service, as soon as a patient is fit to be discharged from Hospital she will if necessary be given 10 days' leave.

(v) On her discharge from hospital, Army Form W. 3016 will be amended as shown in para. 49 (*d*) (i) (ii) and (iii), and will be completed, in triplicate, by the Officer i/c Hospital. One copy will be despatched to the Officer i/c Q.M.A.A.C. Records, one copy to the O.C. or Q.M.A.A.C. Official concerned, and one copy will be retained in the Hospital for reference.

(vi) The O.C. or Official concerned will be responsible for keeping in touch with the Official or Member while on leave; she will issue instructions to her as to time and place of rejoining as soon as the notification of discharge from hospital is received.

It will be stated on A.F. W. 3016 whether the Official or Member is permanently relegated to Home Service only, or, if not, for what period of time. In the latter case at the expiration of the time stated, the Official or Member should be sent to the nearest Receiving Depôt, in order to appear before a Medical Board, which will decide whether she is then fit for service at Home and Overseas.

(vii) In the case of an Official or Member not likely to be fit for further service, she will be brought before an Invaliding Board at the Hospital. A.F. B. 179 will be used for this purpose. If the Board recommend her discharge as physically unfit for further service, A.F. B. 179 will be completed and sent together with Medical History Sheet (A.F. B. 178) to the Officer i/c Q.M.A.A.C. Records, who will record the discharge and notify the same to the Controller of Medical Services. The patient will then be discharged from Hospital and, with due regard to economy, sent to her Accounting Unit for final settlement or to her home. In fixing the date of discharge, the Officer i/c Q.M.A.A.C. Records will take into consideration the conditions of para. 15 (A).

(viii) Officials and Members returned to Hospitals from Overseas, and discharged as " Fit for General Service," will, as a general rule, be drafted again Overseas to the Base Depôt, Q.M.A.A.C. For this purpose, they will be transferred from the Receiving Depôt, London, to the Receiving Depôt for Overseas.

(ix) Officials and Members returned from Overseas who were enrolled subsequent to 6th July, 1917, and who are found fit for Home Service only, will be posted to a Unit at Home, under instructions from the Receiving Depôt, London. If they were enrolled prior to 7th July, 1917, they will be given the option, by the Official concerned of the Receiving Depôt, London, of re-enrolling under these Regulations. If they decline to do so, they must be given one week's notice and discharged.

(x) Officials and Members of the Mobile Branch who make their own arrangements for going into Civil Hospitals or being otherwise treated when sick, will be required to appear before a Medical Board at the nearest Receiving Depôt before resuming work, if their absence from work has exceeded 21 days.

52. SICK LEAVE.

(a) In all cases reference will be made to para. 59 before issuing pay when on Sick Leave.

(b) Sick Leave will be granted by a Medical Board or, for a period not exceeding one month, by any Medical Woman, whose service is authorized in para. 47 (a) (i) and (ii), or by any Officer of the R.A.M.C. The Medical Woman or the R.A.M.C. Officer concerned will send Sick Leave Certificates as follows:—

(i) In the case of Officials to —
   (a) Officer i/c Q.M.A.A.C. Records.
   (b) Headquarters, Q.M.A.A.C.

(ii) In the case of Members to—
   (a) Officer i/c Q.M.A.A.C. Records.
   (b) Official concerned.

(c) If the Medical Board considers it necessary for an Official or Member to appear again before a Medical Board at the expiration of her Sick Leave, she will be instructed by the Medical Board accordingly. If she is given a further extension, Sick Leave Certificates will again be sent as in (b) above.

(d) If at the expiration of her Sick Leave the Official or Member is unfit to appear before a Medical Board, she will send a Medical Certificate to the Official concerned, by whom it will be sent to the President of the Medical Board concerned, who may, at the discretion of the Board, grant a further extension of Sick Leave for a period not exceeding a month at a time.

(e) Cases where Sick Leave is prolonged beyond three months will be reported to the War Office for decision as to whether the Official or Member shall be discharged.

(*f*) (i) In the case of Officials returning home from Overseas on Sick Leave, a certificate stating the duration of Leave will be sent by General Headquarters (Overseas) to the War Office. The Official will normally report for duty to her Unit Overseas on the specified date of return.

(ii) If she is unfit to return, she will report in writing to the Controller of Medical Services, Q.M.A.A.C., War Office, who will arrange for her to appear before a Medical Board. General Headquarters (Overseas) will be notified in such cases by telegram through the usual channels. Sick Leave Certificates will be sent in these cases, as laid down in (*b*) above. General Headquarters (Overseas) will also be advised by telegram through the usual channels of any extension granted.

(iii) The procedure as in (ii) above will be adopted in the case of Officials and Members who fall ill while on ordinary leave from Overseas.

(iv) If an Official or Member on leave from Overseas, is recommended by a Medical Board, to transfer to Home Service for reasons of health, such recommendation will be submitted to Officer i/c Q.M.A.A.C. Records, by the President of the Medical Board.

53. *DISCHARGES ON MEDICAL GROUNDS.*

(*a*) Discharges on medical grounds will be carried out by the Officer i/c Q.M.A.A.C. Records, subject to the recommendations of a Medical Board. All such recommendations, except those forwarded from a Military Hospital, as in para. 51 (vii), will be transmitted to him through the Controller of Medical Services, by whom they will be countersigned. Pending discharge on medical grounds, Officials and Members of the Mobile Branch will be sent, if necessary, to the nearest Receiving Depôt.

(*b*) In exceptional circumstances, where there is special risk or difficulty in bringing her before a Medical Board, the Controller of Medical Services may, at her discretion, recommend the discharge of an Official or Member on a Medical Certificate without referring her to a Medical Board. This will be the usual procedure in the case of Immobile Members. Certificates recommending such discharges will be dealt with as in (*a*) above.

(*c*) Where the Medical Officer in charge of a unit advises the discharge of a Member on medical grounds, he will send a certificate through the usual channels to the D.D.M.S., who will make arrangements through the Assistant Medical Controller for the Member to be brought before the nearest Medical Board of the Q.M.A.A.C.

(*d*) In all cases of discharge of Officials or Members who have served Overseas, A.F. B. 179 will be used.

54. DENTAL TREATMENT.

(a) Dental treatment, but not dentures, will be given when necessary to Members who are about to proceed Overseas, and steps should be taken by the Medical Official of the Receiving Depôt for Overseas to see that all Members who require this treatment receive it before they are sent Overseas.

(b) The above also applies to Members serving Overseas.

(c) Officials serving Overseas may be treated by an Army Dental Surgeon when one is available, otherwise, they will not be provided with dental treatment.

55. SPECTACLES, ARTIFICIAL DENTURES, AND SURGICAL APPLIANCES.

(a) Issues may be made on repayment to Officials and Members employed Overseas of:—
  (i) Spectacles.
  (ii) Artificial Dentures.
  (iii) Surgical Appliances.

(b) Such of the above articles as are included in the "Priced List of Medical Stores, 1917," should be charged at the rates shown therein; the charges for other articles should be assessed locally.

(c) Repairs of these articles may also be effected locally in Army Depôts and Workshops, where facilities exist, on repayment, at fair and reasonable charges.

56. MEDICAL CERTIFICATES.

(a) On transfer, on medical grounds, from "Service at Home and Overseas" to "Home Service only" and vice versa (see para. 13 (c)).

(b) Under arrangements made by Ministry of Labour, (see paras. 40 and 41).

(c) On Change of Category or Sub-Category (see para 21 (D) (vii)).

57. MOTORS.

General Officers Commanding-in-Chief are authorized to provide motor cars for the use of Assistant Medical Controllers on the same conditions as for Controllers (see para. 18 (F)).

58. PROVISION OF NURSES IN Q.M.A.A.C. DEPOTS AND QUARTERS.

(a) In small Quarters, one of the Forewomen should if possible, have had some V.A.D. or nursing experience.

(b) In Quarters of an establishment of 100 or over, an extra Quarters Forewoman, to be called Forewoman Nurse, with some V.A.D. or nursing experience, approved by the Assistant Medical Controller, for this purpose, is allowed in addition to the Quarters Forewomen authorized for general purposes in Appendix B.

(c) In all Receiving Depôts for Home Service, and for Overseas, and in Quarters where the establishment exceeds 500, a trained nurse will be attached. She will receive pay at the rate of £40 for the first year, increasing by £2 10s. per year up to £45 a year, with an extra £20 a year at the end of the first year if she signs for service for the duration of the war, together with board and lodging, and 4s. a week for laundry expenses. She will be entitled to £8 per annum uniform grant, and will not be enrolled in the Q.M.A.A.C., but will be engaged on terms of a month's notice. She will be appointed by the Controller of Medical Services and draw pay and allowances in the manner laid down for Officials. Scale of accommodation will be as laid down in Appendix C, Schedule 6.

(d) In Receiving Depôts for Overseas an extra Quarters Forewoman with some V.A.D. or nursing experience will be appointed as in (b) above.

(e) In Receiving Depôts, and in Quarters of an establishment of over 500, an orderly, Q.M.A.A.C., is allowed for the Trained Nurse or Nursing Sister.

59. *INSURANCE AND PAY DURING SICKNESS, ETC.*

Except as provided below Officials and Members will receive no pay during sick leave.

(A) *Classification, and Eligibility for Insurance.*

For purposes of the National Health Insurance, Officials and Members fall into the following classes:—

Class I. Not Insured at Home or Overseas.

(i) Officials paid at rates in excess of £120 a year.

(ii) Those Officials and Members who were not insured before enrolment and who go Overseas without giving service at Home beyond the training period. If subsequently brought on to Home Establishment they will be reclassified accordingly.

Class II. Insured under Section 47 of the Act at Home (up to 30th June, 1918; subsequently under ordinary provisions), not insured Overseas.

Officials paid at the rate of £120 a year, or less, Members of

Categories "A," "B" (Mobile Branch only*) (*see* para. 21 (C)) and Forewomen and Assistant Forewomen of all Categories.

Class III. Insured under Section 53 of the Act at Home: not insured Overseas.

Employees of G.P.O., except Postwomen.

Class IV. Insured under the general terms of the Act at Home: not insured Overseas.

All other Members, including Category "B." (Immobile Branch).

(B) *Injury or Sickness contracted on Service Overseas.*

(i) Officials whose remuneration exceeds £250 a year will be entitled to the same terms, as regards sick leave and pension, as Medical Women (*see* paragraphs 47 and 48).

(ii) Officials and Members whose remuneration does not exceed £250 a year will receive the following benefits during unfitness:—

(a) *Pay.*

    (i) If injury or sickness is specifically attributable to service Overseas (as certified by a Medical Board); full pay up to a maximum of three months, followed by three-quarters pay for three months, after which, subject to War Office approval, compensation not exceeding half pay will be issuable (*see* (C) (i) below). In all such cases, reference will be made to the War Office if any extension of sick pay beyond the three months on three-quarters pay is required. (*See* Appendix X for detailed instructions)

    (ii) If the injury or sickness is not specifically attributable to service Overseas, full pay up to a maximum of three months will be issuable Overseas. Any extension beyond this period will require War Office approval.

(b) *Hospital Treatment, etc.*

    Free medical attendance will be provided, and hospital treatment where available; no charge will be made to Members in Category "B" (Mobile Branch) (*see* para. 21 (C)). All other Categories will be charged the usual 15*s*. 6*d*. or 14*s*. for board lodging, etc., so long as the charge does not exceed the pay issuable under (B) (ii) (*a*) above.

---

* Members of Category "B" (Mobile Branch only) when drawing sick pay are entitled to the ration and lodging allowance laid down in para. 26 (*b*).

(C) *On return sick from Overseas.*

(i) *Pay and Compensation.*

(a) If the illness is specifically attributable to service Overseas, Officials and Members will continue to be treated as in (B) (ii) or (a) (i) above, periods of service Overseas and at Home being regarded as continuous. If at the end of 6 months from the date of injury or commencement of sickness there is no reasonable possibility of the Member recovering and being able to resume duty, an award of compensation will be made by the War Office, for the duration of the incapacity, at the following rates, viz., where the Member's earning capacity in civil life is shown to have been: —

   (i) Totally destroyed, half earnings not exceeding 25s. a week (this maximum is liable to reduction to £1, six months after the end of the war).
   (ii) Materially impaired, three eighths earnings not exceeding £1, a week.
   (iii) Impaired, one quarter earnings, not exceeding £1, a week.
   (iv) Slightly impaired, one eighth earnings, not exceeding £1, a week.

For further details of compensation, *see* the Scheme framed under the Injuries in War (Compensation) Act, 1914 (Session 2).

(b) If the illness is not specifically attributable to service Overseas, regard is to be had to their position in respect of Insurance (*see* (A) above).

   (i) Class I (excepted from insurance) will receive pay for the unexpired portion of three months (*see* sub-para. (B) (ii) (a) (ii) above).

   (ii) Classes II, III and IV come under the Act.
      Class II (Section 47) will receive up to six weeks' full pay during any period of 12 months from the date of return Home, followed by the usual benefits under the Act.
      Class III (Section 53) will receive two-thirds pay up to three months during any period of 12 months, followed by the usual benefits under the Act.
      Class IV (General Terms of the Act) will receive six weeks full pay from date of

return Home, less 7s. 6d. a week if aged 21 and over, or 5s. if under 21 (followed by usual benefits under the Act).*

(ii) *Medical Attendance and Hospital Treatment.*

Officials and Members may be admitted to the Military Hospital, Endell Street, London, on return from Overseas, or be transferred to a suitable Auxiliary Hospital, where they will remain under treatment until they are physically fit to proceed to their homes. While in hospital deductions will be made from their pay weekly, as follows:—

(a) Officials, when in receipt of pay and insurance benefit of not less than 15s. 6d., will have 15s. 6d. deducted.

(b) Members, when in receipt of pay and insurance benefit of not less than 14s., will have 14s. deducted.

(c) Officials and Members, when in receipt of pay and insurance benefit of less than the above amounts, will have deducted such amounts as they may be in receipt of, but not less than 7s. 6d., if aged 21, or 5s. if under 21.

(d) Category " B," Mobile Branch, will have no deductions made so long as sick pay is issuable. Subsequently, the deduction will be 7s. 6d. or 5s.

(D) *Death following upon Service Overseas.*

In the event of death from injury or sickness specifically attributable to service Overseas, an award under para. (10) of the Scheme framed under the Injuries in War (Compensation) Act, 1914 (Session 2), will be made by the War Office, if the Member leaves any dependants. The total amount of the award will be between £150 and £300 to dependants wholly dependent, or a proportionately smaller sum in the case of partial dependence, subject in either case to reduction by the amount of any injury pay already received on account of the injury or sickness causing death. For details, *see* the scheme.

(E) *Service at Home.*

All Officials and Members serving at Home will be dealt with generally in accordance with the National Health Insurance Act, and the rules laid down in the Regulations for Civilian Subordinates.

---

* Subject to the usual limitation as to not more than six weeks in any period of twelve months.

(i) Officials whose remuneration exceeds £250 a year will be dealt with as above, *i.e.*, they will receive six weeks full pay when sick, except in the event of their having to relinquish their appointments on account of injury or disease specifically attributable to their employment, when they will be eligible for an award under Scale III. of the Treasury Warrant framed under Section I. of the Superannuation Act, 1887 (*see* paragraph 48 (*a*) above for further details).

(ii) Officials and Members whose remuneration does not exceed £250 a year will be called upon as soon as possible after they first join their Unit, to signify in writing on A.F. O.1813 or A.F. O.1813A, their acceptance or refusal of the Scheme of Compensation under the Workmen's Compensation Act, in accordance with paras. 74–6 of the Regulations for Civilian Subordinates (*see* Appendix II. of those Regulations). Controllers will be responsible for seeing that this action is taken in the case of Officials, and the O.C., in the case of all Members, or, in the case of Receiving Depôts, the Official concerned. The Army Forms mentioned above will be forwarded to the Officer i/c Q.M.A.A.C. Records, who will call the attention of O.C. or the Official concerned to the matter when neither Army Form has been received by him within one month of joining. All Officials and Members now serving, who have not made this election, will be required to do so forthwith.

(iii) If injury or sickness occurs which is specifically attributable to their employment as certified by a Medical Board, Officials (with emoluments not exceeding £250) and Members will be entitled to the benefits of the Workmen's Compensation Act or the Scheme in lieu. These benefits and procedure are fully set forth in the Regulations for Civilian Subordinates.

(iv) In the case of sickness not specifically attributable to their employment, the following rules will apply:—

(*a*) *Pay during Sickness.*

   (i) Class I (excepted from Insurance) will receive pay when sick up to six weeks during any period of twelve months.

  (ii) Class II (Section 47) will receive up to six weeks' full pay during any period of twelve months, followed by the usual benefits under the Insurance Act.

 (iii) Class III (Section 53) will receive two-thirds pay up to three months during any period of twelve months, followed by the usual benefits under the Insurance Act

 (iv) Class IV (Others) Members of the Mobile Branch will receive full remuneration as for Class II less 7*s*. 6*d*.

a week if aged 21 and over, or 5s. a week if under 21 (followed by usual benefits under the Act).

Members of the Immobile Branch will receive no sick pay, but the usual benefits under the Act.

(b) Medical attendance and Hospital treatment.

Class I being excepted from insurance will make their own arrangements regarding medical attendance and hospital treatment, except when sick in W.D. Quarters, when they will be treated as under (ii) below.

Classes II, III and IV.

(i) If living in their own homes, will make their own arrangements with a panel doctor under the Act, and will make their own provision for hospital treatment.

(ii) Officials and Members living in W.D. Quarters or Approved Lodgings will make their own provisions for hospital treatment. If they are treated in the Quarters or Lodgings, or in an emergency if it is necessary to send them to a Civil or Military Hospital, they will receive free Medical Attendance and treatment, but the ordinary weekly deductions will be made from their pay, as follows:—

Class I	15s.	6d.
Class II.—Officials... ...	15s.	6d.*
Other Categories (except Category "B" MobileBranch)	14s.	0d.*
Category "B" (Mobile Branch)		nil
Class III	14s.	0d.*
Class IV	14s.	0d.†

* While in receipt of pay in excess of these amounts. Subsequently the actual pay, but not less than 7s. 6d., or 5s. if under 21 years old.

† While sick pay is issuable; subsequently 7s. 6d. (or 5s.). This deduction is in addition to the deduction of 7s. 6d. or 5s. under E iv (a) iv, etc., above; thus a woman whose rate of pay is 24s. weekly would usually draw 2s. 6d. from Army Funds and 7s. 6d. from insurance while sick in Quarters.

(F) *Drugs, Medical Attendance, etc.*

It will be necessary, as in dealing with insured civilian subordinates residing in Government buildings, who receive medical attendance from medical officers of the War Department for the Command Headquarters to enter into negotiations with the local Insurance Committees in the districts in which the Members are employed regarding the amount of the capitation fee to be paid by the Committees to the War Office in return for the drugs, medical attendance, etc., provided for these Members from Army Funds which would otherwise form a charge on the Committee. Immediate steps will be taken by Command Headquarters to secure that the question is taken up in respect of all Members in Quarters or approved lodgings.

(G) *Admittance to Hospital. Charges, etc.*

Headquarters of Commands are responsible that Officials and Members are not admitted to Civil or Military Hospitals except in cases of emergency. They will report to the War Office in cases where accommodation is likely to be inadequate to meet emergencies, with their recommendations to meet the case. Officials and Members will make their own arrangements, when necessary, as to going to a civil hospital, but Command Headquarters should make standing arrangements in advance with local Civil Hospitals in places where the number of Q.M.A.A.C. make this desirable, and fix a suitable charge. In such cases the W.D. will be responsible for paying the Hospital charges, and will recover weekly deductions from the Member as in (E) (iv) (b) (ii) above. This charge will be paid by the Official or Member concerned, unless she has been sent to the hospital in an emergency by the Military Authorities or the Q.M.A.A.C. Official concerned.

These arrangements will not apply to Members of the Immobile Branch.

(H) *Custody of Insurance Cards.*

Officials and Members are responsible for their own National Health Insurance Cards, and Officials are on no account to accept them for safe custody.

(J) *Courts of Inquiry for Injuries.*

In cases where it is considered necessary to hold a Court of Inquiry owing to injury to an Official or Member in the performance of her duty, an Official of the Q.M.A.A.C. and, if it is considered by the Controller to be necessary, an Official of the Medical Services Q.M.A.A.C. will be present to watch the case on behalf of the Q.M.A.A.C.

60. ARREARS OF INSURANCE FOR OFFICIALS AND MEMBERS.

(a) Arrears of insurance covering the period during which Officials and Members have served Overseas will, on their return to this country, be paid out of Army funds.

(b) On transfer of a Member from service Overseas to service at Home, the Official Concerned of the Receiving Depôt for Overseas will ascertain from the Member whether she was insured at the time of proceeding Overseas, and if so, will obtain from the Officer i/c Q.M.A.A.C. Records the date of her embarkation Overseas and of her return to the United Kingdom. She will then stamp an arrears insurance card for the period of the Member's employment Overseas with stamps for the employee's contribution *only*, and will give it to her for transmission to her approved society.

(c) In the case of discharge of an insured Member on return to the United Kingdom, the Official Concerned of the Receiving Depôt will issue the last payment, and will obtain from her the following particulars:—

 (i) Whether she was insured at the time of entering upon Army employ.
 (ii) If so, whether she was a deposit contributor. Otherwise the name and address of her approved society (stating local branch).
 (iii) Her intended place of residence after discharge.

The Official will then obtain from the Officer i/c Q.M.A.A.C. Records the date of the Member's embarkation Overseas and of her return to the United Kingdom, and will stamp an arrears card accordingly, which will be given to the Member for transmission to her approved society.

(d) The statement obtained under (b) and (c) above will be rendered with the pay list in support of the charge of the employee's arrears contributions.

(e) In a case of discharge of an insured Official to the United Kingdom, action as above will be taken by the Command Paymaster, London District.

(f) This arrangement will not apply to Officials or Members whose employment Overseas is terminated by misconduct, and in their cases no arrears of insurance will be paid by the War Department.

61. NATIONAL INSURANCE ACTS (UNEMPLOYMENT).

(a) Unemployment insurance contributions are payable in respect of Members so far as they are engaged on work which falls within the National Insurance (Part II) Act, 1911, and the National Insurance (Part II) (Munition Workers) Act, 1916.

(b) As a guide to those Categories concerned, the following general rules should be noted:—

- (i) The Acts do not apply to Members not engaged wholly or mainly by way of manual labour (a forewoman, for instance, is not engaged on manual labour. Clerks and all persons engaged in writing perform manual *work*, but not manual *labour*).

    No action is therefore necessary in respect of any woman not engaged wholly or mainly by way of manual labour.

- (ii) Members engaged wholly or mainly by way of manual labour are insurable if engaged on certain classes of work, namely:—
    - (a) Manufacture, repair, or inspection of articles intended for use in war. (This will include, for example, Members on fitters' work, doping, fabric work, &c.)
    - (b) In the following trades:—
        Mechanical engineering,
        Construction of vehicles; that is to say, the construction, repair, or decoration of vehicles,
        Sawmilling, including machine woodwork, and other trades not at present affecting Q.M.A.A.C.
    - (c) On custody, handling, packing, or transport of stores in a factory or workshop or in a yard or store *immediately connected* with a factory or workshop wholly or mainly engaged on insurable work.
- (iii) Members engaged on manual labour on classes of work not falling under (ii) are not insurable; *e.g.*, if employed on custody, handling, packing or transport of stores, &c., at depôts not connected with manufacturing establishment they are not insurable.

(c) Where Members are insurable under the Acts reference as to the amount of contributions, &c., should be made to the General Instructions contained in Section XXIII and Appendices VII and VIII of the Regulations for Civilian Subordinates issued with Army Order 223 of 1914. An unemployment book, which can be supplied by the nearest Labour Exchange, should be obtained by each insurable Member, and delivered by her to the O.C. the unit to which she is attached, who will be responsible for the necessary contributions being paid and the necessary deductions being made weekly from the Member concerned. Arrear payments should be dealt with as directed in current A.C.Is.

Reference should be made to current A.C.Is. and to the Regulations quoted above in a case of doubt as to whether any Member is insurable or not, and, if doubt still exists, it should be referred to the Secretary, War Office (F. 6), in which case full particulars of the nature of the work, category of the Member, and place of work, should be stated, and the reason explained why difficulty is found in deciding whether the Member falls under Group (i), (ii), or (iii) of (*b*) above.

APPENDIX A.

Army Form W. 3578.

FORM OF ENROLMENT IN THE QUEEN MARY'S ARMY AUXILIARY CORPS.

No................Name (Mrs. or Miss).........(Christian)...............
      Surname..

Questions to be put to the Woman on enrolment.

1. What is your name?
2. What is your age?
3. What is your permanent postal address?

You are hereby warned that if after enrolment it is found that you have wilfully given a false answer to any of the following questions, the Army Council or any person duly authorized by them retain the right to terminate any contract that they may have entered into with you.

4. Are both your parents British-born subjects?
5. Do you agree to be enrolled in the Queen Mary's Army Auxiliary Corps, and fulfil the rules, regulations and instructions laid down from time to time for this Corps?
6. Are you single, married, or a widow?
7. Have you any dependants?
8. Are you willing to be vaccinated and inoculated?
9. Are you willing to be enrolled for service *(a) at home or abroad; or (b) at home only?

*NOTE.—Strike out (a) or (b).

10. Do you undertake to work wherever the Army Council may require?

†11. Do you undertake to serve in the category, sub-category or grade for which you are selected, or in any other category, sub-category or grade to which you may be transferred or promoted, and to obey all orders given you by your superior officers or those who may be placed in authority over you?

† Category........................ Sub-category........................

12. Do you undertake to perform any work which may be required of you by your superior officers?

13. Do you understand that if at any time in breach of this contract of service you:—

    (a) Without lawful excuse absent yourself from any work

which it is your duty to perform, or from any place where it is your duty to be; or

(b) Refuse or wilfully neglect to perform any of your duties; or

(c) Wilfully impede or delay the due performance of any work on or in connection with which you may be employed;

you will render yourself liable on conviction by a Court of summary jurisdiction to be sentenced to imprisonment with or without hard labour for a term not exceeding six months, or to a fine not exceeding £100, or to both such imprisonment and fine?

14. Do you agree that in the event of being guilty of any act or neglect in breach of this contract or of any of the rules, regulations, or instructions laid down from time to time for this Corps, you will be liable to a Fine:—

On the first occasion of 2s. 6d.
On the second occasion of 5s.
And on the third and every subsequent occasion, of not exceeding 7s. 6d.

15. Do you agree that the decision of the Officer Commanding the military formation to which you may from time to time be attached, that you have rendered yourself liable to any such fine shall be final and conclusive, and shall justify the deduction thereof either in one sum or by any instalments from any wages or other sums due or which may become due to you under this contract: Subject only (in the event of your dissatisfaction with any decision of the aforesaid officer) to any appeal in writing to the Army Council which you may within seven days of the decision of the aforesaid officer hand to such officer for transmission; and that in the event of any such appeal the decision of the Army Council that you have rendered yourself liable to any such fine shall be final and conclusive and shall justify the deduction thereof as aforesaid?

16. Do you agree to serve on the terms and conditions contained in this form and in the Regulations for the Q.M.A.A.C. provided His Majesty shall so long require your services, *i.e.*, for a period of twelve months from .... or for the duration of the war, whichever is the greater period: Provided that your service may be terminated forthwith on ground of misconduct, or breach of conditions, on receipt of notice given by the Army Council or that in the event of your services being no longer required, they may be terminated by one *
notice in writing being given to you?

---

*." Months " ⎱ (according to para. 37 (c) of the Regulations
 " Weeks " ... ⎰   for the Q.M.A.A.C.)

I,............................., do solemnly declare that the above answers made by me to the above questions are true, and I hereby agree to fulfil the engagements made. I have received, read and understand the Regulations for the Q.M.A.A.C. which set forth the conditions of service and rate of pay applicable to me.

..............................*Signature of the Woman.*
..............................*Signature of Witness.*

Medical Classification as to fitness of service on enrolment.
Classification......................
Date..............................191
Place..............................
....
Signature of Medical Officer.

Certificate of Approving Officer.

I approve the enrolment of the above-named woman, and appoint her to be employed with the..............................
Date..............................191 .
Place..............................
....
Signature of Approving Officer.

STATEMENT OF THE SERVICES
OF
No..............Name (Mrs. or Miss)..............................
Christian..............................
Surname..............................

Appointed to	Category and Grade.	Place.	Promotions, &c.	Dates.	Signature of Officers certifying correctness of entries.

Total Service............Years............,Months............Days.

Name and address of next-of-kin..

.... Relationship........................

Particulars as to Children.

Christian Names.	Date.	Place of Birth.

APPENDIX B.

ESTABLISHMENTS.

(1) Details of staff for Receiving Depôts at Home will be authorized as required.

(2) DETAILS OF STAFF FOR QUARTERS AT HOME AND OVERSEAS.

Accommodation.	Permanent Establishment.
A.—50 and under	Deputy Administrator.
B.—50 to 200	Unit Administrator. Assistant Administrator.
C.—200 to 300	1 Unit Administrator. 1 Deputy Administrator. 1 Assistant Administrator.
D.—300 to 400	1 Unit Administrator. 1 Deputy Administrator. †2 Assistant Administrators.
E.—400 to 500	1 Unit Administrator. 1 Deputy Administrator. †3 Assistant Administrators.

(b) *Sick Bay.*

4 per cent. of the accommodation of Receiving Depôts or Quarters at Home will be allowed in addition as a " sick bay " for minor ailments and for isolation purposes.

---

† The extra Assistant Administrators will not be employed until there are at least 50 of the 100 extra Members to be looked after.

(c) *Recreation Room.*

Wherever possible, a suitable room or rooms will be set aside in each Receiving Depôt or Quarters for the purposes of recreation.

(d) *Quartermistresses' Store.*

In Receiving Depôts one room will be fitted up as a Quartermistresses' store.

(3) MAXIMUM PERMANENT ESTABLISHMENTS FOR Q.M.A.A.C. QUARTERS.

Numbers feeding in Quarters.	Forewoman Cooks.	Cooks.	Number in Residence in Quarters.	Quarters Forewoman.	Housemaids, Waitresses or General Domestic Workers.	Number in Residence in Quarters.	Clerks.	Laundry Forewoman.	Laundry women.
1- 20	—	1	1- 10	1	1	1- 20	1	—	1
21- 75	—	2	11- 20	1	2	21- 40	1	—	2
76-175	1	3	21- 30	1	3	41- 60	1	—	3
176-225	1	4	31- 50	1	4	61- 80	1	—	4
226-275	1	5	51- 75	1	5	81-100	1	—	5
276-325	1	6	76-100	1	6	101-120	2	—	6
326-375	1	7	101-125	1	7	121-140	2	—	7
376-425	1	8	126-150	1	7	141-160	2	—	8
426-475	1	9	151-175	1	8	161-180	2	—	9
476-525	1	10	176-200	1	9	181-200	2	1	10
526-575	1	11	201-225	2	9	201-220	3	1	11
576-625	1	12	226-250	2	10	221-240	3	1	12
			251-300	2	11	241-260	3	1	13
			301-325	3	12	261-280	3	1	14
			326-350	3	13	281-300	3	1	15
			351-375	3	13	301-320	4	1	16
			376-400	3	14	321-340	4	1	17
			401-425	4	15	341-360	4	1	18
			426-450	4	16	361-380	4	1	19
			451-475	4	16	381-400	4	2	20
			476-500	4	17	401-420	5	2	21
			501-525	5	17	421-440	5	2	22
			526-550	5	18	441-460	5	2	23
			551-575	5	19	461-480	5	2	24
			576-600	5	20	481-500	5	2	25
			601-625	6	20	501-520	*6	2	26
						521-540	*6	2	27
						541-560	*6	2	28
						561-580	*6	2	29
						581-600	*6	3	30

* One of these may be a Forewoman Clerk.

(4) Forewomen and Assistant Forewomen.

Category Para. 21 (C).	Forewomen.	Assistant Forewomen.	Acting Assistant Forewomen.
A. Clerical	1 to 5*	—	See para. 4. B (ii).
B. Household (i) Cooks	See Appendix B (3) (5) (A) (B) (C) (D) (E).	—	—
(ii) Waitress	See Appendix B (5) (A) (B).	—	—
(iii) Laundresses	See Appendix B (3).	—	—
C. Mechanical	1 to 10	—	—
D. Unskilled	1 to 40	1 to 20	—
E. Telephone and Postal	1 to 20	—	—
F. Miscellaneous	1 to 12	—	—
G. Technical Employments.	1 to 40	1 to 20	—

Os.C. may request in their application for Members that Forewomen may be supplied in the proportion laid down above. The duties of a Forewoman or Assistant Forewoman will be additional to their ordinary duties.

---

* When this proportion is found to be insufficient to replace all the Warrant Officers on the Establishment by Forewomen of the Q.M.A.A.C. a Forewoman may be employed for every Warrant Officer released.

(5) SCALE OF DOMESTIC EMPLOYMENTS IN:—

(A) *Officers' Messes.*

	Up to 25 Officers	From 26 to 50 Officers	From 51 to 100 Officers	From 101 to 150 Officers	From 151 to 200 Officers
Forewoman (Cook).	1	1	1	1	1
Cook	1	2	3	3	4
Vegetable Woman	1	1	1	2	2
General Domestic Workers	1	1	1	1	2

Forewoman (Waitress).—One to each dining room.
Waitresses   } †One for every 8 officers up to 24 officers, 4 for 40
Pantrymaids }   officers and 1 for every additional 10 officers.

(B) *Cadets Battalions.*

EMPLOYMENT.	400	500	600	700
CADET MESS.				
Forewomen Cooks	1	1	2	2
Cooks	8	10	12	14
Vegetable Women	6	7	8	10
Forewomen Waitresses	2	2	2	2
Waitresses	40	50	60	70
Total	57	70	84	98
OFFICERS' MESS.				
Forewomen Cooks	1	1	1	1
Cooks	1	1	1	1
Vegetable Women	1	1	1	1
Forewoman Waitress	1	1	1	1
Waitresses	2	3	3	4
Total	6	7	7	8
SERJEANTS' MESS				
Cook	1	1	1	1
Vegetable Woman	1	1	1	1
Waitresses	3	3	4	5
Total	5	5	6	7

† The proportion of each Category is left to the discretion of the Commanding Officer of the unit.

(B) *Cadets Battalions*—continued.

Employment.	400	500	600	700
MEN'S MESS. Forewoman Cook	—	—	1	1
Cooks	2	2	2	2
Total	2	2	3	3
Totals	70	84	100	116

(C) *Serjeants' Mess.*
Cooks*†.
Pantrymaids†.

(D) *Cook Houses.*
Forewoman (Cook). One to each Cookhouse.

(E) For every 25 or part of 25 above 10 Members of the Household Section (all Categories combined) employed with any one Unit, Depôt or Quarters, one additional Member may be employed, according to the following scale:—

Establishment.	Addition to be allowed.
10–34	1
35–59	2
60–84	3
85–109	4

(F) Cooks will not be required to cut quarters or whole carcases, or to act as stokers. Os.C. will arrange for one butcher and one or two stokers for these duties when necessary.

(G) In officers' and serjeants' messes, where substitution has been effected, the mess serjeant or mess corporal will in all cases be withdrawn and will be replaced, in the case of a N.C.O. employed as mess serjeant, by one Forewoman clerk, and, in the case of a mess corporal, by one Worker clerk. An additional Worker clerk will further be allowed in such cases for every 100, or part of 100, dining numbers in a mess, in excess of the first 100.

(H) Workers will not be employed singly, but in numbers of not less than two in any one formation, and under no circumstances in place of:—
  (i) Batmen.

---

* Where there are over 100 Serjeants in Mess one of the Cooks may be graded and paid as Forewoman Cook.

† The proportion of each Category is left to the discretion of the O.C. of the unit.

(ii) Medical Officers Orderly.
(iii) Regimental Police.
(iv) Butchers.
(v) Quartermasters Storemen.
(vi) Stokers.

(J) Except as laid down above in (3) and (5) above and subject to paragraph (2) D, all Members employed with units serving at Home will be according to the scales laid down for Soldiers in current A.C.Is.

(6) CONTROLLER, DEPUTY CONTROLLER AND AREA MEDICAL CONTROLLER.

One shorthand-typist for each.

(7) RECRUITING CONTROLLER.

One Forewoman Clerk,
One Shorthand-typist,
Two ordinary Clerks,
Two Orderlies,

to be borne on the strength of the Depôt for pay and quarters.

(8) MEDICAL BOARD.

(A) *Permanent.*

One Forewoman Clerk (typist).
One Clerk.
One Orderly (or a second clerk).

(B) *Travelling.*

Two Clerks (to be attached to the Headquarters of a Travelling Medical Board).

APPENDIX C.

EQUIPMENT FOR Q.M.A.A.C. DEPOTS AND QUARTERS.

SCALE OF EQUIPMENT FOR QUARTERS, &c., IN THE UNITED KINGDOM.

(*The Scale of Equipment for Q.M.A.A.C. Quarters Overseas will be laid down by General Headquarters*).

SCHEDULE No. 1.

Controller's, Deputy Controller's, Recruiting Controller's and Unit Administrator's Sitting Room—

Baskets, waste paper 1
Boards, inventory, millboard ... 1

SCHEDULE No. 1—*continued*.

Carpets	1
Chairs, easy, wicker	1
„ rush bottom	1
Curtains, casement cloth, long	1 pair curtains per window where dark blinds are not fitted.

or

Curtains, casement cloth, short	1 per lower half of each window where dark blinds are fitted.
Fenders	1
Pokers	1
Rugs, small	1
Scoops, coal	1
Shovels, fire	1
Tables, tea, small	1
„ writing	1

SCHEDULE No. 2.

Controller's, Deputy Controller's, Recruiting Controller's and Unit Administrator's Bedroom—

Baskets, soiled-linen, round	1
Baths, sitz or sponge	1
Bedsteads, hospital, with spring mattress, complete	1
Bedding (sets)	1 local pattern.
Boards, inventory, millboard	1
Bookshelves	1
Bottles, water, with glass	1
Candlesticks, earthen	2
Cans, water, toilet, 2-gallon	1
Chairs, easy, wicker	1
„ wood	1
Chest dressing, with toilet glass	1
Curtains, casement cloth, long	1 pair curtains per window where dark blinds are not fitted.

or

Curtains, casement cloth, short	1 per lower half of each window where dark blinds are fitted.
Fenders, curb, plain	1 size as required.
Linoleum	As required.
Mats, bath, felt	1
Pails, toilet	1
Pokers	1 where grates with bars are provided.

SCHEDULE No. 2—*continued.*

Rakes, fire	1 where grates without bars are provided.
Rugs, large	1
Shovels, fire	1
Tables, small...	1
Wardrobes	1
Wash-hand stands, complete with ware.	1

SCHEDULE No. 3.

Common Room for Deputy and Assistant Administrators—

Boards, inventory, millboard ...	1
Carpets	1
Chairs, easy, wicker...	1 per three Assistant Administrators.
„ rush bottom	1 „ „ „
Curtains, casement cloth, long ...	1 pair curtains per window where dark blinds are not fitted.
or	
Curtains, casement cloth, short ...	1 per lower half of each window where dark blinds are fitted.
Fenders	1 per grate.
Guards, fire, hanging	1 „
Pokers	1 „
Scoops, coal	1 „
Shovels	1 „
Tables	1
„ writing	1
„ tea, small	1 per 10 Administrators.

SCHEDULE No. 4.

Deputy and Assistant Administrator's Bedroom—

Bedding (sets)	1 local pattern.
Bedsteads, hospital, with spring mattress, complete	1
Boards, inventory, millboard ...	1
Candlesticks, enamelled	1
Cans, water, toilet, 3-quart ...	1
Chairs, wood...	1
Curtains, casement cloth, long ...	1 pair curtains per window where dark blinds are not fitted.
or	
Curtains, casement cloth, short ...	1 per lower half of each window where dark blinds are fitted.

SCHEDULE No. 4—*continued.*

Drawers, chest of, painted	1
Fenders	*1
Glasses, toilet	1
Linoleum or rug or carpet, strips of	As necessary.
Pails, toilet	1
Pokers	°1 where grates with bars are provided.
Rakes, fire	*1 where grates without bars are provided.
Shovels, fire	*1
Towel-horses	1
Tumblers	1
Wash-hand stands, complete with ware.	1

SCHEDULE No. 5.

Unit Administrator's, Deputy and Assistant Administrators scale for 6 occupants—

†*China*—

Basins, slop	1
Bowls, salad	1
,, sugar	1
Cups, breakfast	6
,, egg, china	6
,, tea, china	6
Dishes, butter, common china	2
,, meat, earthen, 14-inch	1
,, ,, 10-inch	2
,, vegetable	2
Drainers, fish, 11-inch	1
Jugs, china, cream	1
,, milk, large	1
,, ,, small	1
Plates, breakfast	12
,, dinner	12
,, soup	6
,, tart	12
Pots, coffee, earthen, 1-pint	2
,, tea, brown, 1-pint	2
Saucers, china, breakfast	6
,, tea or coffee	6
Tureens, earthen, sauce	1
,, ,, soup	1

° Where necessary.

† 25 per cent. of all glass and crockery will be issued to meet breakages.

Schedule No. 5—continued.

† Glass—

Bottles, water, table, 1 quart	2
Dishes, jam	2
Glasses, port	6
Salt-cellars, glass, round	4
Tumblers	18

Cutlery—

Forks, carving	2
,, table, E.P., large	6
,, ,, small	12
Knives, carving	2
,, table, square-handled, large	6
,, ,, small	12
Spoons, E.P., dessert	12
,, salt	4
,, table	4
,, tea	12
Stands, cruet, large	1

Schedule No. 6.

Bedrooms (Women)—

Bedsteads	1 per woman.
Blankets, G.S.	4 per bed.
Boards, inventory, millboard	1
Candlesticks, enamelled iron	1
Cases, slip, pillow	2 per bed.
Chairs, wood	1 per 2 beds.
Curtains, casement cloth, long	1 pair curtains per window where dark blinds are not fitted.
or	
Curtains, casement cloth, short	1 per lower half of each window where dark blinds are fitted.
Drawers, chest of, painted, or double lockers.	1 per 2 beds.
Fenders	*1
Glasses, toilet	1 per 2 beds.
Linoleum	As necessary.
or	
Rugs, small, or carpet, strips of	1 per bed.
Mattresses	1 ,,
Pillows, hospital, hair	1 ,,

* Where necessary.
† 25 per cent. of all glass and crockery will be issued to meet breakages.

Schedule No. 6—*continued*.

Pokers	*1 where grates with bars are provided.
Rakes, fire	*1 where grates without bars are provided.
Sheets	3 per bed.
Shovels, coal, small	*1
Towel-horses	1 per 2 beds.
Towels, Turkish	3 per woman.
Tumblers or mugs, ½-pint	1 per bed.
Wash-hand stands, complete, with ware (where no washing accommodation is provided)	1 per 2 beds.

Schedule No. 7.

Dining Halls—

Boards, inventory, millboard	1
Brushes, hearth	1 per grate.
Fenders	1
Forms, dining, tent, 6 feet	1 per four women.
Pokers	1
Scoops, coal	1
Shovels, fire	1
Tables, portable, F.S., 6 feet	As necessary.

Pimlico Section—No. 30—

Forks	1 per woman.
Knives	1 ,, ,,
Spoons	1 ,, ,,

Schedule No. 8.

Recreation Rooms (Women)—

Boards, inventory	1
Chairs, easy, wicker	1 per 10 women.
,, wood	1 ,, 10 ,,
Couches, tapestry covered	1 ,, 100 ,,
Covers, table	1 per table.
Curtains, casement cloth, long	1 pair curtains per window where dark blinds are not fitted.
or	
Curtains, casement cloth, short	1 per lower half of each window where dark blinds are fitted.
Fenders	1
Forms, portable, F.S., 6 feet	As necessary.
Linoleum	,,
Pokers	1 per grate.
Rugs, Axminster	1 ,,

* Where necessary.

Scoops, coal ...	1 per grate.
Shovels, fire ...	1
Tables, portable, F.S., 6 feet	As necessary.

SCHEDULE No. 9.

Ablution Rooms—

Baths (where no fixed baths are provided).	1 per room.
Forms, dining tent, 6 feet ...	1 ,,
Pails, slop, enamelled, with lid	1 per 50 women.

SCHEDULE No. 10.

Office—

Baskets, waste paper	1 per administrator.
Boards, inventory, millboard	1
Boxes, cash, G.S.	1 for Depôt Hostels only.
Chairs, Windsor	1 per Administrator and clerk.
Fenders, curb, plain...	1 per grate.
Hods, coal ...	1
Pokers	1 per grate.
Rugs, hearth...	1 ,,
Shovels, fire ...	1 ,,
Tables	1 per Administrator (if necessary).
,, soldiers'	As necessary for clerks.
Tongs...	1

SCHEDULE No. 11.

Sick Room and Surgery (as for Bedroom, Women, with the following additions)—

Basins, washing, earthen	1 per 5 beds.
Boxes, dressing	1 per room.
Brushes, bed pan	1 ,,
Feeders, earthen	1 ,,
Jugs, enamelled iron	1 per 5 beds.
Kettles, tea ...	1 per 10 beds.
Measures, glass, 4-oz.	1 per room.
,, ,, 2-oz.	1 ,,
Pans, bed, earthen ...	As necessary.
Screens, bedside	2 per room.
Sheets...	1 per bed.
Tables, pedestal, bedside	1 per room.
,, portable, F.S.	1 ,,
Thermometers, common	1 ,,
Trays, diet, 10 diet...	1 per 100 women.
Warmers, stomach ...	1 per room.
Wash-hand stands, japanned, complete with ware ...	1 ,,

Schedule No. 12.

Kitchen and Scullery—

Basins, pudding, enamelled	12 per 100 women.
Baskets, hand	2
Bins, ash, movable	As necessary.
Boards, chopping, 2 feet	1
" inventory	1
" pastry	2
" knife	1
Boxes, brush	1
" coal	1 (size as necessary).
" spice	1
Bowls, hand	1 per 20 women.
" mixing	2 " 50 "
Brooms, bass	2
Brushes, polishing	2
" flue	2
Canisters, japanned (7 lbs.)	3
Cans, 3 gallons, with lids	2 per 100 women.
Choppers, meat, 10-inch	1
Colanders, tin, 16-inch	2 per 100 women.
Corkscrews	1
Dishes, baking, tinned, iron	As necessary.
Dishes, meat, earthen	1 per 8 women.
" pie	1 " 8 "
" vegetable, plain	1 " 8 "
Forks, cooks'	2
Graters, bread	1 per 150 women.
Implements, butchers', hooks, dressing	2
" " choppers	2
" " saw, tenon	1
" " steels	1
Jugs, earthen, large, 4 quarts	6 per 100 women.
" " shipshape	6 " 100 "
" " small	6 " 100 "
Kettles, fish, tin	1 " 100 "
" tea, 10 quarts	1 " 24 "
" " 2 quarts	1 " 100 "
Knives, cooks, 9-inch	2 " 100 "
" " 6-inch	2 " 100 "
" opening tins	1
Ladles, cooks', barrack	2
Machines, mincing, tinned iron, large	1
" weighing, 28 lbs., spring balance	1
Machines, bacon slicing	1 per every 250 women in mess.
" bread cutting	1 per every 250 women in mess.

SCHEDULE No. 12—*continued.*

Kitchen and Scullery—continued.

Mops, common, complete	...	2
Pails, iron, galvanised, 3 gallon	...	2 per 100 women.
Pans, frying, large, 16-inch	...	1 ,, 100 ,,
,, ,, medium, 8-inch	...	1 ,, 100 ,,
Pins, rolling	...	2
Pokers, soldiers'	...	1
Pots, coffee, 4 pints	...	4 ,, 100 ,,
Saucepans, enamelled, 1 quart	...	1 ,, 100 ,,
,, iron tinned, 6 quarts	...	1 ,, 100 ,,
,, ,, 4 ,,	...	1 ,, 100 ,,
,, ,, 2 ,,	...	1 ,, 100 ,,
Shovels, fire, soldiers'	...	1
Skewers, sets of 12	sets	1 per 100 women.
Slicers, fish	...	1 ,, 50 ,,
Spoons, gravy	...	2 ,, 100 ,,
,, wooden, large	...	1 ,, 100 ,,
,, ,, small	...	1 ,, 100 ,,
Strainers, wire, 15-inch	...	1
Tables, portable, F.S., 6 feet	...	As necessary.
Trays, tea, large	...	2 per 100 women.
,, medium	...	2 ,, 100 ,,
,, small	...	2 ,, 100 ,,
Tubs, washing, 3½ gallons	...	2
Whisks, egg	...	1

SCHEDULE No. 13.

Linen, &c.—

Cloth, American	...	As necessary for mess tables.
Cloths, glass	...	30 per 100 women.
Dusters	...	10 ,, 100 women.
Towels, hand	...	3 per bed.
,, round	...	2 per ablution room ; 4 per sick room ; 8 per kitchen.

SCHEDULE No. 14.

China—

Basins, slop	1 per 16 women.
Boilers, tea or coffee	1 per 24 women.
Bowls, sugar	1 per 16 women.
Cups, tea, earthen (Serjeants' Mess)	1 per head and 10 per cent. spare.
Dishes, meat, earthen, 14-inch	1 per 8 women.
,, ,, 10-inch	1 ,, ,,
Plates, dinner	2 per head and 20 per cent. spare.

Schedule No. 14—*continued.*

China—continued.

Plates, soup	1 per head and 10 per cent spare.
,, tart	1 per head and 10 per cent. spare.
Saucers, tea	1 per head and 10 per cent spare.
Tureens, earthen, sauce	1 per 16 women.
,, ,, soup	1 ,, ,,

Glass—

Bottles, water, table, 1 quart	2 per 8 women.
Tumblers	1 per woman and 5 per cent. spare.

Cutlery—

Forks, carving	1 per 20 women.
Knives, carving	1 ,, ,,
Spoons, table	1 per 4 women.
,, tea	1 per head.
Stands, cruet, large	1 per 8 women.

Schedule No. 15.

Miscellaneous—

Axes, felling	2
,, hand or hooks, bill	4
Bells, hand, 1 lb.	1
Bins, ash, movable	1 per floor of building.
Blocks, chopping	1 per butcher's shop.
Brushes, blacklead, round	1 per floor of building.
,, ,, stove	1 ,, ,,
,, closet	1 per lavatory.
,, hand, hard	1 per floor of building (if necessary).
,, scrubbing, hand	2 per floor of building.
,, sweeping, hand	1 ,, ,,
,, ,, long	1 ,, ,,
Buckets, fire	As necessary.
Chisels, ripping	1 where necessary.
Clocks, horizontal	1
Guards, fire	1 per fire-place in Q.M. store.
Hammers, coal	4 where necessary.
,, claw, 16-oz.	1 ,, ,,
Ladders, step, 10 feet	1

SCHEDULE No. 15—*continued.*

Miscellaneous—continued.

Lamps, hurricane	...	4 where necessary.
Mats, coir fibre, door	...	1 per outside entrance door.
Mops, common	...	1 per floor of building.
Nailpullers	...	1 where necessary.
Pans, dust	...	1 per floor of building.
Pails, iron, 4 gallons	...	2 ,, ,,
Screwdrivers, G.S., 9-inch	...	1
Tubs, washing, 3½ gallons	...	1 per floor of building.

Implements, Butcher's—

Cleavers, 2 ft. 1 in.	...	1
Hooks, dressing	...	6
Saws, tenon, 14-inch	...	1
Steels	...	1

} For butcher's shop.

SCHEDULE No. 16.

Recruiting Board—Stationery, &c.—

Stationery ... as necessary { To be demanded from the Secretary (C. 2) War Office.

SCHEDULE No. 17.

Recruiting Board—Furniture, &c.—

Baskets, waste paper	2
Boxes, index, card	6
Chairs, wood	6
Cupboards, lock-up	1
(If necessary ; size as required.)	
Fenders	...*—
Linoleum	...*—
Pokers (where grates with bars are provided)	...*—
Rakes, fire (where grates without bars are provided)	...*—
Shovels, fire	...*—
Tables, with drawers to lock	2
Tables, wood, plain	4

SCHEDULE No. 18.

Selection Board—Furniture, &c.—

Baskets, waste paper	2
Chairs, wood	12

* Where necessary.

SCHEDULE No. 18—*continued*

Selection Board—Furniture, &c.—continued.

Fenders	*—
Forms, wood, 6 feet	4
Linoleum	*—
Pokers (where grates with bars are provided).... ...	*—
Rakes fire (where grates without bars are provided) ...	*—
Shovels, fire	*—
Tables, wood, plain	4

SCHEDULE No. 19.

Medical Board—Army Forms, Stationery, &c.—

Army Book 46 (Medical register) as required	⎫
Army Test types ... ... sets 1	
Army History Sheets (Army Form W. 3661) for each day ... 150	⎬ To be demanded from the Secretary (C. 2), War Office.
Instruction for Physical Examination of Recruits (Army Order 273 of 1914.	
Medical History Sheets (A.F. B. 178) 150	
Regulations for the Army Medical Service. 1	
Stationery ... ... as necessary	⎭

SCHEDULE No. 20.

Medical Board—Medical Stores—

Carbolic lotion, 1 in 20 ... pints 2	⎫
Depressor, tongue, glass 1	
Fork, turing, plain pattern ... 1	
Speculum, Auris, Brunton's ... 1	
Stethoscope, binaural 1	⎬ To be obtained from the D.D.M.S. of the Command.
Tapes, measuring, mounted ends ... 2	
Test types, sets on cards, reading ... 1	
Tray, dressing, enamelled steel, 11″ × 9″ × 2″ 1	
Trial case of test lenses, unmounted, small 1	⎭

SCHEDULE No. 21.

Medical Board—Furniture, &c.—

Baskets, waste paper	2
Blankets, G.S.	3

* Where necessary.

SCHEDULE No. 21—*continued.*

Medical Board—Furniture, &c.—continued.

Brushes, nail	2
Chairs, wood	24
Couches, examination, with pillows	1
Cupboards, lock-up (if necessary, size as required)	1
Dusters	6
Fenders	*—
Forms, wood, 6 feet	1
Kettles, for hot water, 2-pint	1
Machines, weighing, man	1
Mirrors, small	1
Pails, slop	1
Pokers (where grates with bars are provided)	*—
Rakes, fire (where grates without bars are provided)	*—
Rugs	2
Screens, fourfold	12
Shovels	*—
Standards, measuring, height	1
Tables, wood, plain	3
,, writing	3
,, ,, with drawers	1
Towels	12
Tumblers	1
Wash-hand stands, japanned, complete, with ware	1

APPENDIX D.

SCALE OF RATIONS.

(1) RATIONS FOR THE Q.M.A.A.C. AT HOME.

Meat—7 ozs. (as an alternative, meat 5 ozs.; bacon, 2 ozs.).
Bread—11 ozs.
Tea—⅜ oz.
Sugar—1¼ oz.
Salt—¼ oz.
also 6½d. commuted ration allowance.

---

* Where necessary.

(2) RATIONS FOR Q.M.A.A.C. OVERSEAS.

Meat	... 8 ozs.	Bread	...	11 ozs.
Bacon	... 2 ozs.	Margarine	...	1 oz.
Potatoes	... 8 ozs.	Jam	...	3 ozs.
Fresh Vegetables	... 4 ozs.	Sugar	...	2 ozs.
Salt	... $\frac{1}{4}$ oz.	Milk	...	2 ozs.
Pepper	... $\frac{1}{100}$ oz.	Cheese	...	1 oz.
Mustard	... $\frac{1}{100}$ oz.	Rice or Oatmeal	...	2 ozs.

Tea $\frac{1}{2}$ oz. or Coffee 1 oz. or Cocoa 1 oz.

APPENDIX E.

ACCOUNTING INSTRUCTIONS.

1. Accounting arrangements will be governed by Army Regulations generally. For details not herein provided for see the Regulations for Civilian Subordinates issued with Army Order 223 of 1914.

I.

OFFICIALS OF THE Q.M.A.A.C.

Home and Overseas.

2. The Army Agents are in no way concerned with the issue of pay to Officials of the Q.M.A.A.C., and application will on no account be made to them.

3. Officials serving at Headquarters will be paid under War Office arrangements.

4. Other Officials serving at Home, including Probationers under instruction at a Training Centre and Officials on duty at a Depôt preparatory to proceeding Overseas or to another Home station, will be paid by the Command Paymaster of the Command in which they are serving at the end of the month.

5. Pay will be claimed on A.F. O.1679. In the case of Controllers A.F. O.1679 will be signed by a Staff Officer of the Command Headquarters. In the case of other Officials, it will be signed by the O.C. the Unit to which Quarters are attached, or the Senior Official of the Receiving Depôts, or the Area Controller, or a Staff Officer of the Command Headquarters, as may be convenient.

6. If an Official is transferred to another station (at Home or Overseas) other than from the 1st of the month, she will take with her A.F. O.1679, which will show the particulars as in paragraph 9 or 10 in regard to the part of the month spent at the first station, and will be certified as regards that period by one of the Officials specified in paragraph 5. The pay, being issuable at the end of the month only, need not be assessed for the broken periods separately.

7. Officials serving Overseas will be paid by the Command Paymaster at the Base. Their claims will be signed as in paragraph 6 so far as it applies.

8. Outfit grants will be claimed from the Command Paymaster, as laid down in paragraph 19 of the Q.M.A.A.C. Regulations.

9. Where the Official is entitled to free quarters it will be shown on A.F. O.1679 at what Depôt or Quarters, &c., she was accommodated.

10. Claims for lodging allowance under paragraph 26 of the Q.M.A.A.C. Regulations will be made on A.F. O.1679, and will be supported by a certificate that accommodation in a W.D. Depôt or Quarters was not and could not be obtained.

11. On receipt of a notification in Part II. Orders of the transfer of an Official to a station in another Command, the Command Paymaster who has dealt with her claim for pay for the month preceding transfer, will immediately forward a last pay certificate to the Command Paymaster of the new station.

12. The Command Paymaster who issues an Official's pay for any period of service in another Command will notify to the other Command Paymaster concerned the period for which rations and commuted allowances may be allowed for the Quarters in which the Official was accommodated before transfer, certifying at the same time that the corresponding deduction has been made from her pay. The certificate will be placed with the accounts at the Quarters.

13. The National Health Insurance cards of an insured Official who is serving at a Home station will be stamped by the Command Paymaster from whom she draws her pay. If desired, the Command Paymaster will retain the card until the termination of the insurance period or until the Official is about to proceed Overseas, when he will return it to her.

14. The pay and allowances of Medical Women appointed for duty with the medical services of the Q.M.A.A.C. will be adjusted as laid down in paragraphs 47 and 50 of the Q.M.A.A.C. Regulations.

II.

MEMBERS: AT HOME.

Pay.

15. Members serving in the United Kingdom will be paid as follows:—

    (a) Members serving with Units or Formations, or on the Staff of Quarters, by the O.C. Unit to which they are attached, or such O.C. Unit as may be selected by the G.O.C.-in-C. or G.O.C.

    (b) Members on the strength of Receiving Depôts by the Officials concerned.

16. In all cases the pay lists will be rendered to the Command Paymaster of the Command in which the Unit or Depôt or Quarters is stationed.

17. Where Members are attached to a Unit for payment, it is desirable that the Officer responsible for the pay list should be a sub-accountant of the Command Paymaster. No Officer may hold simultaneously two imprests; therefore in regimental formations it should be arranged, where practicable, that an Officer other than a Company, &c., Commander shall be made responsible for the payment of the Members and the preparation of their pay list. So far as possible such Officer should not be below the rank of Captain.

18. Where the Members have to be paid by an Officer who is a sub-accountant of a Regimental Paymaster, they will be paid from that Officer's Regimental imprest, but the pay lists will be rendered to the Command Paymaster, who will remit the allowed expenditure by draft. In such case the amount due from the Command Paymaster at the end of the account period will be entered as a separate item in the Cash Reconciliation Statement.

19. Officials of Receiving Depôts will obtain imprests from the Command Paymaster.

20. The amounts paid to the Members will be claimed and imprests (in cases other than those referred to in paragraph 15 above) will be accounted for on A.F. W. 3994, supplies of which should be indented for as required.

Note.—Until supplies of A.F. W. 3994 are available, A.F. N1504 or N.1510 should be used.

21. The amounts chargeable against the public in the pay list are:—

    (a) The pay, gratuity, and clothing upkeep grants actually issued to Members.

(b) Sums charged against Members in respect of clothing, &c., issues on repayment.

(c) The Members' and the Army Council's insurance contributions.

(d) Contingent allowance, where admissible.

(e) Ration and lodging allowance paid to Members under paragraph 26 (b) of the Q.M.A.A.C. Regulations.

(f) The cost of railway tickets under paragraph 18 (C) of the Q.M.A.A.C. Regulations.

(g) Charges for approved lodgings under paragraph 22 (G) (ix) of the Q.M.A.A.C. Regulations.

Note.—The commuted allowance for rations is chargeable in the pay list of the Unit Depôt or Quarters by which Officials or Members are rationed, *see* paragraph 25 of the Q.M.A.A.C. Regulations.

22. Pay will be issued weekly in arrear. Payment will ordinarily be made on Friday or Saturday, the weekly emoluments being assessed up to Friday inclusive.

23. Pay for broken periods and stoppages of pay for absence will be adjusted on the basis of one-seventh the weekly rate for each day in the period.

24. When a Member is transferred to the payment of another Unit at Home, the paying Officer who has kept her account will settle with her to the last Friday before she joins the new Unit, and will credit her account in the pay list with pay to that date only. Where, however, the Member is transferred late in the pay week, a reasonable cash advance may be made to her, and this will appear on the last pay certificate as a debtor balance on transfer.

25. When a Member is transferred Overseas, her account will be closed as indicated in paragraph 21 (F) of the Q.M.A.A.C. Regulations. The amount of the advance will appear as a debtor balance on the last pay certificate and will also be recorded in the pay book (A.B. 64). The pay book will be shown as opening on the date following that to which the pay prior to embarkation has been reckoned, under paragraph 21 (F) of the Q.M.A.A.C. Regulations.

26. For every Member who is transferred to other payment the paying Officer will prepare a last pay certificate on A.F.W. 3994, and will forward it to the Command Paymaster for transmission to the Member's new paying Officer or the Command Paymaster, Base, as may be necessary.

27. The first charge of pay in the account of the new Unit will be supported by the last pay certificate.

28. Fines will be recovered by debit in the column provided for the purpose in the pay list, and deduction from current issues of pay.

29. The gratuity for Members of the Mobile Branch will be payable on the last Friday in each quarter, the first payment in a Member's service consisting of a proportionate amount at the rate of 1s. for each complete week's service in the Mobile Branch; and a proportionate amount similarly calculated will be payable up to the date of death in the service, discharge (for any cause other than misconduct or breach of conditions) or up to the date of transfer to the Immobile Section (*see paragraph* 13 (*b*) of the Q.M.A.A.C. Regulations). The first quarter commenced as from 29th December, 1917, the first quarterly payment being due on the last Friday in March, 1918.

Where the quarter includes sick leave or leave in excess of that for which pay is issuable, the gratuity will be assessed at 1*s.* per week on the number of weeks' service with pay.

Rations.

30. Where Members are attached to Army units for rations, *see* paragraph 25 (*b*) of the Q.M.A.A.C. Regulations, their rations will be indented for by the Unit. Rations drawn for Members of the Q.M.A.A.C. will be shown separately on A.F. F.743. The Unit's claim for the rations and for the corresponding number of days' commuted allowance will be supported by A.F. P.1950, which will be rendered with the pay and mess book of the Company by which the Members are rationed.

31. In other cases rations will be indented for by the Official responsible for feeding the Members and A.F. F.743 for rations issued to Depôts or Quarters will be rendered to the Command Paymaster.

32. For the day on which a Member is transferred from one Unit to another, a money allowance of 1*s.* 2*d.* will be drawn instead of the ration and the allowance referred to in 30 above. The charge will be made in the account in which the commuted allowance for the Member has been previously claimed, and an adjustment will be made between the Units, Depôt or Quarters concerned, as laid down in A.C.I. 238 of 1917.

33. The Official concerned, in charge Depôt or Quarters, by which Members are rationed will obtain funds on imprest from the Command Paymaster, and will render to that Officer an account in which she will charge the commuted allowance referred to in 30 above, together with any money allowance admissible under paragraph 32 above, and will account for all rations drawn. The account will be rendered by account periods (ending on the last Friday in each month). With it

will be furnished a statement of the number of days' commuted allowance, and money allowance under paragraph 32 above, and will be supported by the pay list of each Unit the Members of which have been accommodated at the Depôt or Quarters, &c., during the account period. The Command Paymaster will check the charges by comparison with claims on Army Form O.1679 for pay of Officials and the pay lists rendered by the paying Officers.

34. The Official concerned of each Receiving Depôt or Quarters will keep an account in Army Book 48 of the expenditure of the commuted allowance and any money allowance for rations drawn under paragraph 32 above. The account will be audited by the Messing Auditor of the Command, to whom the Command Paymaster will furnish the usual return on A.F. W.3176.

35. Overdrawals and underdrawals of rations will be adjusted in accordance with paragraph 53, Allowance Regulations.

III. MEMBERS: OVERSEAS.

36. The pay accounts of Members serving Overseas will be kept on A.F. W.3085 by the Command Paymaster, Base.

37. The Members will be paid on the acquittance roll (A.F. N.1513), all issues being recorded in the pay book (A.B. 64). Cash issues will be made in the currency of the country in which the Members are serving.

38. Gratuities and clothing upkeep grants as they become due will be noted on page 3 of the pay book. Credit to the Members' accounts will be given by the Command Paymaster as the grants accrue.

39. Repayment issues under paragraph 55 of the Q.M.A.A.C. Regulations will be adjusted on similar lines.

IV. GENERAL.

Classification.

40. Charges for pay, insurance, gratuities to the Mobile Section, outfit allowance and clothing and upkeep grants will be classified to Vote 1.W.B. Charges for travelling allowances and expenses and money allowances in lieu of rations or accommodation will be charged to ordinary votes.

41. Command Paymasters at Home will adjust the classification by posting to headings other than Vote 1.W.B. such portion of the paying Officer's cash issues as equals the credits in the pay lists of sums chargeable under those heads, the

balance only of the cash issues being charged against Vote 1.W.B.

42. The Command Paymaster, Base, will make the necessary classification adjustment by charging the Vote concerned and crediting Vote 1.W.B. when he credits a Member's ledger account with any sum chargeable against a head of service other than Vote 1.W.B.

Travelling Claims.

43. Travelling claims will be rendered to the Command Paymaster for payment to the Official or Member concerned.

Contingent Allowance.

44. For the Contingent allowance drawn under paragraph 22 (E) of the Q.M.A.A.C. Regulations, a separate account will be kept, containing full particulars of the expenditure of the allowance. The balance on this account will be kept separate from the balance on the imprest account. The account will be produced for inspection when required.

APPENDIX F.

A.F.W. 3631

CONSOLIDATED RETURNS.

A.F.W. 3620A for each unit will be attached to this return in all cases where Members are accommodated in Depôts or Quarters.

*Consolidated returns of Q.M.A.A.C. (other than Officials) required in the .... Command during the month of ....

Unit for which required.	Nearest Railway Station.	Nature of Accommodation (see back).	Date by which Accommodation will be ready.	Permanent staff required, vide Appendix B.	Numbers required.	Is uniform admissible (see back)?	Occupation vide Appendix B.

Place.................... Date.................... Signature....................

HOME SERVICE.

Uniform will be worn at Home only by Members of the Q.M.A.A.C. whose duties necessitate their regular attendance at Military Camps or Barracks.

ACCOMMODATION.

A. Accommodation for Members in their own homes.
B. Quarters.
C. Lodgings. (Under Q.M.A.A.C. Approved Lodging s Scheme.)

Note.—Lodgings are not permissible without special sanction from the War Office.

APPENDIX G.

M. 40/13.

ACKNOWLEDGMENT OF ENROLMENT.
Q.M.A.A.C.
Selection Board.

....

This is to state that.. is enrolled in the Q.M.A.A.C.

for { *Home Service only*

Home or Overseas as from (date). ....

The applicant must hold herself in readiness to present herself for service on that date. Full information as to the date or the place at which she is to report will be sent later.

(Sgd.) ....

(President of Selection Board.)

(To be handed to candidate after interview by Selection Board.)

APPENDIX H.

M. 40/14.

NOMINAL ROLL.
Ref. No................ Q.M.A.A.C.

Nominal Roll of Members to be posted to .... on................

Name.	Postal Address.	Occupation (see Schedule).	Rate of Pay.	Station.	Time of Arrival.	Remarks.

Place ....
Date............... .... Signature.......................................

N.B.—This form should be sent to arrive at least three clear days before Members are due to arrive at Depôts or Units.

APPENDIX J.

A.F. W. 3632.

RESULT OF SELECTION AND MEDICAL BOARDS FOR Q.M.A.A.C. HELD AT.................ON..................., 19......

(To be posted to Officer i/c Q.M.A.A.C. Records on the completion of each Board.)

SUMMONED.			NET RESULT.
A.	*Home.*	*Overseas.*	
(1) Accepted by Selection Board	....	....	....
(2) Failed to appear	... ...	... ...	....
(3) Withdrawn voluntarily	... ...	... ...	....
(4) Rejected by Selection Board...	... ...	...	....
B.	*Home.*	*Overseas.*	
Submitted by Selection Board to Medical Board :—			....
(1) Passed by Medical Board	....	....	....
(2) Deferred	...	... ...	....
(3) Rejected by Medical Board ...	...	... ...	....
Occupation.	*Home.*	*Overseas.*	
....	....	....	....
....	....	....	....
Total	Total	Grand Total	

Date.......................... Signed..........................

Net Result. Occupation.   Overseas.   Home.

....

Total ......

Signature ....
Date........................

APPENDIX K.

M.40/9.

Application No.

For *Official use only*.   CONFIDENTIAL.

FORM OF APPLICATION FOR ENROLMENT.—
MOBILE BRANCH.

N.B.—No woman need apply who is not prepared to offer her services for the duration of the war and to take up work wherever she is required.

1. Name in Full (Mrs. or Miss)	2. Permanent Postal Address
3. Surname at birth, if different	

4. In what capacity do you offer your services? (The occupations and rates of pay are set out in para. 21 (C) of the Regulations for the Q.M.A.A.C.)

5. Are you willing to serve :—
   (*a*) At Home and Overseas as may be required
   (*b*) At Home only

6. If selected and enrolled how many days' notice will you require before your services are available?

7. Age and date of birth	8. Place and Country of Birth
9. Nationality at Birth	10. Present Nationality (if naturalised give date)
11. Whether single, married or widow If married state number of children (*a*) under 12 years old (*b*) ,, 5 ,,	12. If not single state Nationality of Husband. (*a*) Is your husband serving with the Forces? (*b*) If so, where?
13. Father's Nationality at Birth	14. Mother's Nationality at Birth

15. Father's Occupation

16. State school or college where educated.
    At what age did you leave school?

17. Particulars of any other Training, stating Certificates held.

18. (*a*) Name and Address of your present employer (*see Note at end*)
   N.B.—(The employer will not be referred to unless he is given as a reference under paragraph 20 below.)
   (*b*) Nature of his business
   (*c*) Capacity in which you are employed
   (*d*) Length of your service with him
   (*e*) Salary which you are now receiving

19. Previous business experience (if any) giving dates, salaries received, and names of Employers

20. Give below for purposes of reference the names of two or more British householders with their permanent addresses, one of whom should be, if possible, your present or previous Employer, a Teacher, a Town Councillor, Mayor or Provost, Justice of Peace, Minister of Religion, Doctor or Solicitor, who has known you for two or more years, but is not related to you. One of the references must be a woman.

   (*a*) Name
   Profession or Occupation
   Address
   (*b*) Name
   Profession or Occupation
   Address
   (*c*) Name
   Profession or Occupation
   Address

An offer of Service can in no way be regarded as a final enrolment.

I hereby declare that the above statements are complete and correct to the best of my knowledge and belief.

Date   Usual Signature

This Form should be filled in by the Applicant and returned to :—
EMPLOYMENT EXCHANGE,

....

NOTE.

Women who are already engaged in any of the following occupations will not be accepted unless they bring with them a letter from their Employer or Head of Department stating that they have permission to volunteer :—
   (i) All Government Departments (including the War Office and Military Pay Offices at Home but excluding all other military offices).
   (ii) Establishments (other than military units) under the control of the War Office.
   (iii) Forces of the Overseas Dominions except as agreed with their respective Headquarters.
   (iv) Munition factories.
   (v) Controlled firms.

(vi) Voluntary Aid Detachments. Military Hospitals or Red Cross Hospitals.
(vii) Schools (teachers).
(viii) Municipal services, or municipal industrial undertakings.
(ix) Firms engaged on Government contracts.
(x) Agriculture.

APPENDIX L.

M. 40/9A.

Confidential.
Application No.
For Official use only.

FORM OF APPLICATION FOR ENROLMENT FOR IMMOBILE BRANCH OF Q.M.A.A.C.

N.B.—No woman need apply who is not prepared to offer her services for the duration of the War.

1. Name in full (Mrs. or Miss).
2. Permanent postal home address.
3. Surname at birth, if different.

4. In what capacities do you offer your services? (The occupations and rates of pay are set out in para. 21 (C) of the Q.M.A.A.C. Regulations.)

5. If selected and enrolled, how many days' notice will you require before your services are available?

6. Age and date of birth.
7. Place and country of birth.

8. Nationality at birth.
9. Present nationality. (If naturalised, give date).

10. Whether single, married or widow.
    If married, state number of children—
    (*a*) under 12 years old;
    (*b*) under 5 years old.
11. If not single, state nationality of husband.

12. Father's nationality at birth.
13. Mother's nationality at birth.

14. Father's occupation.

15. State name of school or college where educated. At what age did you leave school?

16. Particulars of any other training, stating certificates held.

17.—(a) Name and address of your present employer (*see* Note at end).

> *N.B.*—The employer will not be referred to unless he is given as a reference under para. 19 below.

(b) Nature of his business.
(c) Capacity in which you are employed.
(d) Length of your service with him.
(e) Salary which you are now receiving.

18. Previous business experience (if any), giving dates, salaries received, and names of employers.

19. Give below for purposes of reference the names of two or more British householders, with their permanent addresses, one of whom should be, if possible, your present or previous Employer, a Teacher, a Town Councillor, Mayor, Provost, Justice of the Peace, Minister of Religion, Doctor or Solicitor, who has known you for two or more years, but is not related to you.

One of the references must be a woman.

(a) Name.   (c) Name.
Profession or occupation.   Profession or occupation.
Address.   Address.
(b) Name.
Profession or occupation.
Address.

An offer of service can in no way be regarded as a final enrolment.

I hereby declare that the above statements are complete and correct to the best of my knowledge and belief.

Date .... Usual Signature ....

This form should be filled in by the applicant and returned to :—

Note.—Women who are already engaged in any of the following occupations will not be accepted unless they bring with them a letter from their employer or head of department stating that they have permission to volunteer :—

- (i) All Government Departments (including the War Office and Military Pay Offices at Home but excluding all other military offices).
- (ii) Establishments (other than military units) under the control of the War Office.
- (iii) Forces of the Overseas Dominions (except as agreed with their respective Headquarters).
- (iv) Munition factories.
- (v) Controlled firms.
- (vi) Voluntary Aid Detachments. Military Hospitals or Red Cross Hospitals.
- (vii) Schools (teachers).
- (viii) Municipal services, or municipal industrial undertakings.
- (ix) Firms engaged on Government contracts.
- (x) Agriculture.

No woman who is a National Service Volunteer or is employed in agriculture will be accepted.

N.B.—Applicants are urged not to give up any present employment until they are called upon to do so.

Space for Official use only.

Application received on ....

by ....

Forwarded on .... by ....

APPENDIX M.

RECEIPT FORM FOR APPLICATION FOR ENROLMENT.

M. 40/10

Ministry of Labour,
Employment Exchange,
......................Date.

Your offer to serve in the Queen Mary's Army Auxiliary Corps has been duly received and will be carefully considered. *A further communication will be addressed to you in due course.* Should you in the meantime change your address you should notify this change to this Employment Exchange. You are strongly urged not to leave any work in which you may be at present engaged until you are asked to do so.

Sgd................................Manager.

APPENDIX N.

REFERENCE FORM.

M. 40/11.

Ministry of Labour,
Employment Exchange,

..............19...

Urgent and Confidential.

To..................................

Mrs. }
*Miss } ....

residing at ....
has recently applied for enrolment in the Queen Mary's Army Auxiliary Corps and has given your name as reference. I shall be obliged if you will kindly reply to the questions overleaf, and return this letter to me at your earliest convenience. Your replies will be treated confidentially and will not be communicated to the above applicant. An addressed envelope is enclosed for your convenience.

Sgd. ....Manager.

Questions.

1. How long have you personally known applicant and in what capacity?
2. What do you know of applicant's qualifications as............... and how are you qualified to speak for her?
3. Do you know applicant to be:—
    (a) Steady and reliable?
    (b) Industrious?
    (c) Thoroughly discreet and trustworthy?
4. Is applicant to your knowledge a fit person to be trusted with access to documents of a confidential nature?
    Note.—This question need not be answered *except* in the case of clerks, typists or like occupations.
5. Do you know applicant to be a British subject?
6. Was applicant born a British subject?
7. What was the nationality of applicant's father at his birth?
8. What was the nationality of applicant's mother at her birth?
9. If married, what was the nationality of applicant's husband at birth?

To the best of my knowledge and belief the above answers are correct.

Signature ....
Occupation or profession..........................

---

* Surname at birth, if different, should also be given.

APPENDIX O.

Army Form W. 3629

CANDIDATE'S FORM OF SUMMONS.

Miss }
Mrs. } ....
Address..

YOU ARE REQUESTED to attend at (Place).......................
on (date)...........................at (hour)...........................with a view to being considered for selection as a Member of the Q.M.A.A.C. in accordance with your application dated.........

If approved by the Selection Board and passed fit by the Medical Board you will be enrolled and will be posted for duty accordingly.

If accepted for service you will not be required to report for duty before the date on which you inform the President of the Selection Board you will be available.

Full instructions regarding the place and date of joining will be sent in due course.

* A return Railway Warrant for the journey is enclosed. (If for any reason you are unable to attend you should communicate with.. and should return the Railway Warrant.)

Signature...................................

* To be struck out if the candidate does *not* reside more than five miles from the place of meeting of the Selection Board.

APPENDIX P.

Army Form W. 3630.

CALLING UP NOTICE.

Mrs. }
Miss } ....

With reference to your enrolment for service in the Queen Mary's Army Auxiliary Corps you are hereby ordered to present yourself at...............................on...........................

Full instructions for your journey are given below and a Railway Warrant is enclosed.

You should bring all necessary underclothing with you and your luggage should consist of a small handbag or parcel only; it is suggested that you provide yourself with a rug.

If for any unforeseen reasons you are unable to travel on the day mentioned you should at once communicate with

....

Signature..................................

Directions for journey.

You are to leave....................................Station by the train leaving at................................and to travel to.....................Station, at which you will arrive at................................ You will be seen off at*..............................by...........................
met at............................by...........................

If not met at the station you should proceed to...................

* Strike out if no arrangements for seeing off are made.

APPENDIX Q.

M. 40/15.

REFUSAL OF APPLICANT.

....Selection Board.

....191

DEAR MADAM,

I am desired by the Selection Committee for the Q.M.A.A.C. to inform you that they have carefully considered your application for service in the Corps, they regret, however, that they are unable to accept you for enrolment.

Yours faithfully,
(Signed)

Clerk to the Selection Board.

APPENDIX R.

A.F.W. 3620A.

APPLICATION FOR OFFICIALS* FOR THE PERMANENT STAFF OF AND INFORMATION CONCERNING THE Q.M.A.A.C. QUARTERS IN WHICH MEMBERS REQUISITIONED WILL BE ACCOMMODATED.

Notes.

PART 1.—OFFICIALS.

Command .... Unit to which Quarters is attached .... Postal Address of Quarters.............................	Type of Quarters.*	Total number of members employed† and living in the Quarters. †

Grade of Official.	Establishment.	Employed at present.	Now required.	Is uniform admissible.	Certified that the accommodation for the Officials requisitioned has been inspected and found satisfactory and will be ready for occupation on .... Signed............ .... Senior Area Controller.
UNIT ADMINISTRATORS ..					
DEPUTY " ..					
ASSISTANT " ..					

This space for War Office use only.

................Appointed as............. ..on............... ....Appointed as...............on............... ....Appointed as...............on...............	Received in War Office.	M.S. Ref. No.

* *Vide* Appendix " B " (2) of Q.M.A.A.C. Regulations.
† Inclusive of Permanent Staff.

PART 2.—INFORMATION CONCERNING QUARTERS.

ostal Address of Quarters.......................... earest Railway Station				Type of Quarters (A, B, C, D, or E).*	
rmy Units§ to which Members are attached for work.	Address of Army Units.	Number employed† by each Army Unit.	Number employed‡ and entitled to uniform *vide* Q.M..A.A.C. Regulations.	Present Maximum Accommodation.	
				Date on which Hostel is ready for occupation.	
				For War Office use only.	
				Required for .... and................................. R. and F......................	
				A.G. XI. Ref. No.	
'ERMANENT STAFF.					

* *Vide* Appendix "B" (2) of Q.M.A.A.C. Regulations.
† Inclusive of Permanent Staff.
‡ Inclusive of Outstanding Requisitions Unfilled.
§ The actual Unit with which the Members are working should be shown ; it is not sufficient to state merely the Command, Garrison, Division or Brigade.

Command............................ Signed............................
Date ....

APPENDIX S.

MEDICAL CERTIFICATE.
(Immobile Branch.)

Strictly Confidential.   Serial Number.........

1. Name..........................   3. General Health...............
2. Address......................   4. Is her vision good?...........
5. Is her hearing perfect?...
6. Are her teeth sound?..
7. Does she suffer from any form of fits?...............................
8. Is she suffering from any of the following diseases:—
   (a) Heart Disease. (b) Varicose Veins. (c) Tuberculosis.
9. Is she suffering from any form of infectious skin disease?
10. Has she been exposed to any infectious disease within the last 21 days?...
11. Is she, in your opinion, in a suitable condition of health for regular employment in...
12. Is she, in your opinion, suitable for work in respect of:—
    (a) Personal cleanliness.
    (b) General Health.

I have, on the............day of.....................191..., seen and examined... and hereby certify that she is, as recorded above, apparently in good health, that she is not labouring under any deformity, and is, in my opinion, both physically and mentally competent to undertake work in a................................

                 Signed..
Date.........................   Address.......................................

APPENDIX T.
APPOINTMENT, TRANSFER, PROMOTION AND DISCHARGE OF OFFICIALS.

1. *APPOINTMENT.*

    (A) *Direct Appointments of Officials.*

    (i) At the completion of the probationary period, A.F.W. 3662 will be forwarded by Headquarters, Q.M.A.A.C., to the War Office for approval and gazette.

    (ii) The following documents will be kept by the Officer i/c Records:—

    A.F. W. 3662 with approval of appointment;
    Record of Service Sheet;
    Medical Schedule;
    Identification Certificate.

(iii) Headquarters, Q.M.A.A.C., will notify the Controller concerned when an Official is being posted to a Command.
(iv) The Controller will notify such posting to the G.O.C.-in-C. or G.O.C. of the Command.

(B) *Appointment of Officials from Members of the Q.M.A.A.C.*
- (i) If recommended by the Official and the O.C. concerned, A.F. W. 3662 will be completed by the Candidate.
- (ii) A.F. W. 3662 will then be sent to the Controller concerned, who will arrange to interview the Candidate.
- (iii) The Controller, if she considers the Candidate suitable, will forward A.F. W. 3662 together with covering letter, to the Chief Controller, Headquarters, Q.M.A.A.C.

  If the Candidate is serving Overseas, this will be passed through G.H.Q.

  If the Candidate is serving at Home, she will be ordered to attend a course of lectures for Officials in training, and a 3rd class Railway Warrant will be issued for the journey.

  If the Candidate is serving Overseas, she will be transferred Home for training.
- (iv) If recommended by the Chief Controller, her papers will be sent to the War Office for approval and gazette.
- (v) All former documents dealing with the Candidate's record of service (except her enrolment form A.F. W. 3578) will be transferred from the Q.M.A.A.C. Record Office and kept at Headquarters, Q.M.A.A.C.
- (vi) Her other documents will be dealt with as in 1 (A) (ii) above.

2. *TRANSFERS WITHIN A COMMAND.*
(i) With the concurrence of Command Headquarters, Controllers may carry out transfers within the Command, notifying such transfers to Headquarters, Q.M.A.A.C.

3. *TRANSFERS FROM ONE COMMAND TO ANOTHER.*
- (i) These will be carried out by Headquarters, Q.M.A.A.C., who will notify Controllers concerned.
- (ii) Controllers will, in all cases, notify G.O.C. of Commands concerned, who will instruct the O.C. the unit that the transfer is to be made.

4. *CONFIDENTIAL REPORTS.*
(i) In the event of an adverse report being made by an

Official or an O.C., it will be shown to and signed by the Official reported on, who may sign a statement if she desires, which will be attached.

Such reports will be forwarded through Command Headquarters to the War Office, together with the remarks of the Controller, and a recommendation as to the disposal of the case. No Official will be discharged for any reason without War Office sanction.

5. *RECOMMENDATIONS FOR PROMOTION.*

(i) These will be forwarded by Command Headquarters at Home, and G.H.Q. Overseas, to the War Office, together with the remarks of the Official and the Commanding Officer concerned.

6. *DISCHARGES.*

Discharges of Officials will generally be dealt with on the lines laid down for Members (para. 15 of the Q.M.A.A.C. Regulations), except that they will be carried out through the ordinary official channels by the War Office and not by the Officer i/c Q.M.A.A.C. Records.

APPENDIX U.

ARMY FORMS ONLY APPLICABLE TO Q.M.A.A.C.

W.3620A. Application for Officials, &c.
3662. Application Form for Officials (formerly A.G.XI/194).
3630. Calling Up Notice (Supply held by Ministry of Labour).
3629. Candidates' Form of Summons (Supply held by Ministry of Labour).
3677. Character Certificate.
3578. Enrolment Form.
3683. Depôt or Quarters Daily Strength Return.
3680. Depôt or Quarters Description Card.
3577. Identification Certificate.
3674. Landlady's Receipt.
3675. Leave of Absence Pass.
3661. Medical Schedule.
3631. Monthly Return.
3626. Receipt Card for Clothing.
3646. Record Card.
3625. Requisition for Clothing.
3632. Results of Selection, &c.
3682. Return of Draft.
3994. Pay List.

Army Form W. 3677.

APPENDIX V.

CHARACTER CERTIFICATE.

WARNING.—*If you lose this Certificate a duplicate cannot be issued.*

N.B.—*Any person finding this Certificate is requested to forward it to the Officer i/c Records, Q.M.A.A.C., c/o the Secretary, War Office, S.W.1.*

1. QUEEN MARY'S ARMY AUXILIARY CORPS.
Character on discharge of No _____
Name _____
Grading _____
Enrolled at _____ on _____
Discharged _____ on _____

2.   WORK.
Her work during the time she has been in the Corps has been
_____
                  Signature _____
Date _____

3.   PERSONAL CHARACTER.
Her personal character during the time she has been in the Corps has been _____
                  Signature _____
Date _____   [P.T.O.

Description of No. _____
_____ Queen Mary's Army Auxiliary Corps
Age _____
Height _____
Build _____
Eyes _____
Hair _____
                  Signature _____
Date _____

Marks or Scars, whether on face or other parts of body.

APPENDIX W.

DISCHARGE CERTIFICATE.

WARNING.—*If you lose this Certificate a duplicate cannot be issued.*

> Certificate of discharge of No._____
> (Name) _____
> Queen Mary's Army Auxiliary Corps_____
> who was enrolled at_____
> on the_____ 19
>
> She is discharged in consequence of_____
>
> (Place)_____
> (Date)_____
> Signature of Officer i/c }
> Records, Q.M.A.A.C.   } _____
>
> Description of the above-named woman on discharge :
> Age_____   Marks or Scars, whether on face
> Height_____   or other parts of body :
> Build_____
> Eyes_____
> Hair_____

N.B.—*Any person finding this Certificate is requested to forward it to the Officer i/c Q.M.A.A.C. Records, War Office.*

APPENDIX X.

DETAILED INSTRUCTIONS AS TO THE APPLICATION TO MEMBERS OF THE Q.M.A.A.C. OF THE SCHEME No. (1) FRAMED UNDER THE INJURIES IN WAR (COMPENSATION) ACT, 1914 (SESSION 2).

INJURY OR SICKNESS.

(1) *While the Member remains Overseas.*

Immediately a Member becomes unfit for her employment

from any cause, the O.C. will fill up Sections (A) and (B) of I. in W. Form No. W.1., and forward it to the Medical Officer of the Hospital to which the Member is being or has been sent, for completion of the Medical Certificate (C). On return of the form from the Hospital, the O.C. the Unit will complete Section D. of I. in W. Form No. W.1., in accordance with the following instructions:—

(a) If the injury arose out of, and in the course of the Member's employment Overseas, or if the sickness is certified by the Medical Officer as specifically attributable to the nature and conditions of such employment, as the case may be, the O.C. will award injury pay at the rate of full pay for a period not exceeding 3 months, or the period of unfitness estimated by the Medical Officer, whichever is less. If, at the end of 3 months, the Member is still unfit, I. in W. Form No. W.2. will be completed, and a further award of injury pay at the rate of three-quarters full pay will be made for a further period not exceeding 3 months. If at the end of 5 months, the Member is still Overseas, and is likely to be unfit for a period exceeding 6 months in all, I. in W. Form No. W.3. will be completed and forwarded to the War Office (F.3.) through the usual channels, together with copies of any previous reports on Forms W.1. and 2. Further awards will be made by the War Office in accordance with the terms of the Scheme. Os.C. should prepare such copies of the above forms as may be necessary to enable them to keep a complete series for each case for purposes of reference.

(b) If the injury did not arise out of and in the course of the employment Overseas, or if the sickness is certified by the Medical Officer to be not specifically attributable to the nature and conditions of such employment, sick pay at the rate of full pay may be awarded, while the Member is obliged to remain Overseas, for a period not exceeding 3 months, provided that the injury or sickness was not attributable to the Member's serious and wilful misconduct.

(2) *When the Member is sent back to the United Kingdom.*

In the case of Members entitled to treatment under either (1) (a) or (1) (b) above, I. in W. Form No. W.3. will be at once filled up, and forwarded to the War Office through the usual channels.

APPENDIX XA.

INSTRUCTIONS AS TO THE PAYMENT OF INJURY PAY UNDER THE WORKMEN'S COMPENSATION ACT TO OFFICIALS AND MEMBERS OF THE Q.M.A.A.C. IN CASES WHERE WOMEN ARE INJURED BY ACCIDENT IN THE COURSE OF THEIR EMPLOYMENT AT HOME.

Injury while on Home Service.

Attention is drawn to the following:—

Any Official or Member meeting with an injury, however trivial it may seem, in the execution of her duty, should immediately report the circumstances to the Official or subordinate Official over her. A certificate on A.F. O. 1664 will be prepared and forwarded as soon as possible to the Medical Officer, who will examine the Official or Member, and will on the Army Form describe the injuries sustained, and show, as far as the nature of the case will permit, whether it appears to have resulted from the accident as stated. This Army Form will be used as a sub-voucher to support the *first* charge for Injury Pay (if admissible) in the Pay List. Subsequent charges will be supported by a reference to the Authority for the *first charge*, and medical certificates at reasonable intervals, as to continued incapacity arising from that injury.

Attention is also drawn to the necessity of:—

(i) Either making the Payment of Injury Pay due under paragraph 80 of the Regulations for Civilian Subordinates where the incapacity resulting from the injury and the circumstances under which the injury by accident is such as to render Injury Pay admissible, *or*

(ii) Reporting immediately to the War Office (F.6.) under paragraph 90 of the Regulations for Civilian Subordinates, such report being accompanied by A.F. O.1664. It should be noted that certain increases in the rate of Injury Pay over those shown in paragraph 81, Regulations for Civilian Subordinates are payable during *total incapacity* (*see* AC.Is. 1505 and 1607 of 1917).

APPENDIX Y.

Q.M.A.A.C. UNIFORM.

Annual Issues for Mobile Branch.

Articles.	Clerical Section.	Domestic Section.	Motor Drivers' Section.	Unskilled Members and Storewomen.	Postal Section.	Miscellaneous Section.	Technical Section.
Coat frock	1	1	—	1	1	1	1
Coat	—	—	1	—	—	—	—
Skirt, lined	—	—	1	—	—	—	—
Collars	3	3	3	3	3	3	3
Gaiters ... pr.	1	1	—	1	1	1	1
Greatcoat (on first issue only)	1	1	—	1	1	1	1
Hat	1	1	1	1	1	1	1
Overalls	2	4	—	2	2	2	2
Shoes ... pr.	1	1	1	1	1	1	1
Stockings	2	2	—	2	2	2	2
Badges, sets (on first issue only)	1	1	1	1	1	1	1
Numerals ... sets	1	1	1	1	1	1	1
Greatcoat, warm M.S. (on first issue only)	—	—	1	—	—	—	—
Brassard (on first issue only)	1	1	1	1	1	1	1

Conditional Issues for Mobile and Immobile Branches.

(Issuable in addition to the above Annual Issues at the discretion of Commands at Home and G.H.Q., Overseas.)

Articles	Clerical Section.	Domestic Section.	Motor Drivers' Section.	Unskilled Members and Storewomen.	Postal Section.	Miscellaneous Section.	Technical Section.
Boots, gum ... pr.	1	1	1	1	1	1	1
Clogs ... ,,	—	1	—	—	—	—	—
Aprons, rubber	—	1	1	—	—	—	—
Waistcoats, Cardigan	—	—	—	—	—	1	—
Boots, heavy ... pr.	—	—	1	—	—	1	—
Breeches ... ,,	—	—	1	—	—	1	1
Caps, leather	—	—	1	—	—	—	1
Coats, rubber	—	—	—	—	—	1	—
Gloves, driving ... pr.	—	—	1	—	—	—	—
Goggles ... ,,	—	—	1	—	—	—	—
Hats, waterproof	—	—	—	—	—	1	—
Jerkin	—	—	1	—	—	—	—
Overalls, washing	—	—	2	—	—	—	2
Overalls	—	—	—	2	—	—	—
Leggings, leather pr.	—	—	—	—	—	1	—
Tunic or Smock	—	—	—	—	—	1	—

Annual Issues for Immobile Branch.

Brassard 1	
Overalls 2	For all Sections
Caps (where necessary) 2	
Numerals, Sets 2	

Renewal Grants for Mobile Branch.
(Issuable at the commencement of the second six months of each year.)

	£	s.	d.
Motor Drivers' Section : Forewoman	2	10	0
Worker	1	10	0
All other Sections	1	0	0

APPENDIX Z.

Repair of Shoes belonging to Members of the Corps.

On and after 1st April, 1918, the repair of shoes belonging to Members will be carried out in Command Repair Depots as under:—

Command or District.	Repair Depôt.
Scottish	Stirling.
Northern	Halifax.
Western	Halifax.
Eastern	Old Kent Road, London.
London	Old Kent Road, London.
Southern	Southampton.
Aldershot	A.O.D. Workshop, Field Stores, Aldershot.

2. Shoes for repair, securely tied together in pairs, each pair labelled, with the name of the owner, will be collected by Administrators, or Deputy Administrators, who will despatch them in bulk, packed in sacks or other convenient packing, to the Repair Depôt concerned.

3. Each consignment should, in addition, contain a list signed by the Administrator showing the names of the owners of the shoes and the address to which they are to be returned after repair for distribution to the owners.

4. Carriage of the shoes from the collecting centre referred to in para. 2 to the Command Repair Depôt and from that Depôt to the distributing centre referred to in para. 3 will be a charge against the public, but the individual Member will defray any carriage charges which may be incurred in sending the shoes to the collecting centre, or from the distributing centre after repair.

5. Charges for repairs will be made on the following scale:—

Full repairs, to include washing, oiling, repairing, examination, packing, labour and materials:—

With Hobnails.

Half-soles only	2s. 9d. per pair.
Heels only	1s. 0d. ,,
Full repair	3s. 9d.

Without Hobnails.

Half-soles only	2s. 6d. per pair.
Heels only	10d. ,,
Full repair	3s. 4d.

Minor Repairs additional.

Stitching seams and replacing eyelets	3d. per pair.
Buckles or straps	3d. each.
Patches, according to size, from	3d. each.

Shoes will *not* be hobnailed without special instructions.

The foregoing charges are subject to periodical revision.

6. The Officer i/c a Repair Depôt, when returning the repaired shoes, will furnish the Administrator with a statement of the amounts to be recovered from the owners. The Administrator will recover the amounts due from the women concerned and forward to the Command Paymaster, through the O.C. the Army unit with which the Member works, the original list of charges received from the Repair Depôt, as a voucher for the credit to the public.

7. This will not apply to Officials.

APPENDIX ZA.

SCALE OF CAMP EQUIPMENT.

ADMINISTRATORS, DEPUTY AND ASSISTANT ADMINISTRATORS.

SCHEDULE No. 1.—ADMINISTRATOR'S OFFICE.

Section No. 2a.

Lanterns, tent, folding	1
Tents, C.D.L. with wood bottoms	1 per camp.

Section No. 11.

Stools, serjeants	2
Tables, soldiers, 4 ft. complete ...	1

SCHEDULE No. 2.—ADMINISTRATOR'S ACCOMMODATION.

Section No. 2a.

Lanterns, tent, folding	1 per tent.
Tents, C.D.L. with wood bottoms	1 per 2 Administrators.

Section No. 11.

Chairs, Windsor	1 per Administrator.
Cups, tea	1 per Administrator.
Glasses, looking, hospital	1 per tent.
Plates, breakfast	1 per Administrator.
Plates, dinner	2 per Administrator.
Saucers, tea	1 per Administrator.
Washhand stands, hospital, iron, complete with ware.	1 per tent where lavatory accommodation is not provided.

Section No. 13a.

Blankets, G.S.	3 per Administrator.
Bolsters, barrack, coir	1 per Administrator.
Cases, slip, bolster, barrack, coir ...	1 per Administrator.
Mattresses, S.S.	1 per Administrator.

Section No. 13b.

Bedsteads, folding, Mark II ...	1 per Administrator.

Section No. 13c.

Towels, Turkish	2 per Administrator.

Pimlico Section No. 30.

Forks	2 per Administrator.
Knives	2 per Administrator.
Spoons	2 per Administrator.

WOMEN.

Schedule No. 3.—Sleeping Accommodation.

Section No. 2a.

Bedsteads, F.S.	1 per woman.
Lanterns, tent, folding	1 per tent.
Tents, C.D.L. with wood bottoms	1 per four women.
Tubs, washing, 3½ gallons	2 per tent.

Section No. 11.

Glasses, looking, hospital ... 1 per tent.

Section No. 12.

Pails, iron, galvanized, 3 gallons ... 1 per tent where lavatory accommodation is not provided.

Section No. 13a.

Blankets, G.S.	3 per woman.
Cases, bolster	1 per woman.
Cases, paillasse	1 per woman.

Section No. 13c.

Towels, Turkish ... 2 per woman.

Schedule No. 4.—Dining and Recreation Room.

Section No. 2a.

Forms, dining, tent	As necessary.
Kettles, camp, oval	1 per 8 women.
Lanterns, tent, folding	4 per tent.
Stoves, Soyers	1 per camp of 60 women or over (if necessary).
Tables, dining, tent	As necessary.
Tents, store	1 per camp of 60 women and over up to 150 (if necessary).

Section No. 11.

Brooms, bass or birch	4 per camp of 60 women.
Mugs, enamelled	1 per woman.
Plates, dinner	2 per woman.

Section No. 12.

Cans, 3 gallons	3 per dining tent.
Dishes, meat, tin, 17½ in.	As necessary.
Tubs, washing, 8 gallons	2 per dining tent.

Pimlico Section No. 30.

Knives	1 per woman.
Forks	1 per woman.
Spoons	1 per woman.

INDEX.

ACCOMMODATION— PAGE.
    Allowances, contingent ... 43
    Barrack damages ... 44
    Camps, Summer ... 45
    Depots, Receiving ... 42
    Hutments ... 45
    Immobile branch ... 42
    Lodgings ... 44, 46
    Mobile branch ... 42
    Quarters ... 42
        Equipment ... 85
        Establishment ... 80
    Washing household linen ... 43
    Works services ... 41
ACCOUNTING—
    Instructions ... 98
    Pay ... 41
    Uniform ... 29
        Overseas ... 32
ADMINISTRATION ... 9
ADVERTISEMENTS—
    Recruiting ... 50
ALIENS—
    Enrolment of ... 50
ALLOWANCES—
    Contingent ... 43
    Fuel and Light ... 46
    Lodging ... 47
    Ration ... 47
    Travelling ... 24
        Medical services ... 62
APPLICATION FOR OFFICIALS FOR PERMANENT STAFF ... 116
APPOINTMENT—
    Officials ... 10, 118
BADGE—
    Silver, on discharge ... 20
BARRACK DAMAGES ... 44
BOARD—
    Lodging, service, and washing ... 46
CABS—
    Hiring of ... 23
CALLING-UP NOTICE ... 114
CAMPS, SUMMER—
    Accommodation, etc. ... 45
    Equipment, scale of ... 45, 128

CERTIFICATES—	PAGE.
Discharge	122
Character on	19, 121
Medical	66, 118
CLOTHING—*See* Uniform.	
COMPENSATION—	
Service at home, sickness or injury due to	70
Service overseas—	
Death following upon	70
Injury or sickness from	68
CORRESPONDENCE—	
Letters	13
Telegrams	13
DEFINITIONS	7
DENTAL TREATMENT	66
Artificial dentures	66
DEPÔTS—	
Receiving	42
Equipment for	85
Establishments for	80
DISCHARGES	18
Badge, silver on	20
Certificate	122
Character on	19, 121
Compassionate	18
Immobile members	19
Inefficiency	18
Medical grounds	18, 65
Misconduct, breach of conditions	19
Notice of	18, 19
Officials	120
Termination of, by notice	19
Uniform of discharged members	30
DISCIPLINE	12
DOCUMENTS	13
ENROLMENT	51
Debarred from—	
Reserved occupations	49
Temporarily	50
Forms	77
Acknowledgment of	106
Application for	108, 110
Immobile branch	110
Mobile branch	108
Receipt form	112
Immobile Branch—	
Women already employed in the Army	55
Women not already employed in the Army	54
Mobile Branch	51, 108
Re-enrolment existing personnel into	48
Travelling expenses, prior to, on joining, on termination	23
Women already employed in Army	55
EQUIPMENT—	
Camps, Summer	45, 128
Quarters and depôts	85

	Page
ESTABLISHMENTS—	
Details	80
EXCHANGES	16
FORMS—	
Army forms only applicable to Q.M.A.A.C.	120
Candidate's form of summons	114
Enrolment. *See* Enrolment.	
Reference	113
FUEL AND LIGHT—	
Allowances for	46
FUNERALS	48
GRATUITY—	
Medical women	60
Mobile branch	32
HOSPITALS—	
Admission to	62
Charges, etc.	73
Treatment, insured members	70, 72
HOTELS—	
Charges	26
HUTMENTS	45
IDENTITY DISCS	30
IMMOBILE BRANCH	8
Accommodation	42
Discharges	19
Enrolment, form of application for	110
Leave of absence pass	21
Medical certificate	118
Movements of personnel	17
INJURIES —	
Court of Inquiry for	73
Injuries in War, Compensation Act	122
Medical women, gratuity or pension for	60
See also Insurance and Pay during Sickness.	
Workmen's Compensation Act	124
INSTITUTES, REGIMENTAL—	
Use of	47
INSURANCE AND PAY DURING SICKNESS	67
Arrears of	74
Cards, insurance, custody of	73
Drugs, medical attendance	73
Home service	70
Hospitals, admittance to, charges, etc.	73
Injuries, Courts of Inquiry for	73
National Insurance Unemployment Act	74
Overseas	68, 69
LABOUR, MINISTRY OF—	
Responsibilities regarding recruiting for Q.M.A.A.C.	53
LEAVE—	
Absence without	21
Allowances, ration and lodging on paid	47
Deductions during	47
Pass for leave of absence	21

	PAGE.
LEAVE—*continued.*	
Pay—	
With	20
Without	21
Sick leave	64
LETTERS	13
LIGHT—	
Allowances for	46
LODGINGS	44, 46
Allowances	47
MEAL, STANDARD—	
While travelling	26
MEDICAL—	
Attendance, drugs, etc., insured member	73
Boards	61, 107
Certificates	66, 118
Dental treatment	66
Discharges on medical grounds	65
Hospitals, admission to	62
Insurance and pay during sickness	67
Nurses, provision of, for Q.M.A.A.C. quarters, depôts	66
Sick leave	64
Spectacles, artificial dentures, surgical appliances	66
MEDICAL SERVICES—	
Boards, medical	61
Gratuity	60
Motors for	66
Officials	58, 59
Organization	57
Pay, rates of	59
Pension	60
Travelling allowance	62
MOBILE BRANCH—	
Accommodation	42
Enrolment—	
Form of application for	108
Re-enrolment, existing personnel into	48
Women already employed in Army	55
Gratuity for	32
Leave of absence pass	21
Movements of personnel—	
Home	16
Overseas	17
Officials must join	11
Organization	7
Travelling facilities	22
MOTOR CARS—	
Use of, by Controllers	23, 66
MOVEMENTS OF PERSONNEL—	
Immobile branch	17
Mobile branch—	
Home	16
Overseas	17

	PAGE.
NOMINAL ROLL	106
NUMBERS—	
Allotment of	15
NURSES—	
Pay	67
Provision of, in Q.M.A.A.C. Quarters and Depôts	66
OBJECT	8
OFFICIALS—	
Appointment	10, 118
Discharge	120
Duties, domestic, technical	11
Grades	10
Medical services	57, 58, 59
Mobile branch, must join	11
Pay, issue of	40
Promotion	120
Subordinate	12
Transfer	119
ORGANIZATION—	
Immobile	8
Mobile	7
OUTFIT. *See* Uniform.	
PAY—	
Accounting, method of	41
Additional categories	41
Advance of	41
Basis of	32
Deductions from	41
Increases	39
Initial rate of	39
Injury	122, 124
Issue of	40
Leave	20, 21
Mobile branch, gratuity for members	32
Nurses	67
Rates of	33
Medical services	59
Sickness, pay during	67
Transfers, pay on, and authority for fixing	39
PENSIONS—	
Medical women	60
POSTINGS	16
PROMOTIONS	15
Officials	120
QUARTERS (mobile branch)	42
Equipment	85
Establishment	80
Receiving	42
RAILWAY WARRANTS. *See* Travelling.	
RANK—	
Officials	10
Sub-officials	12

	Page
RATIONS: At home and overseas—	
Allowance	47
Scale	46, 97
RECORD OFFICE	18
RECRUITING—	
Advertisements	50
Aliens	50
Enrolment forms	50
Immobile branch	54, 55
Mobile branch	51, 55
Reserved occupations	49
REDRESS	20
REFERENCE FORM	113
REFUSAL OF APPLICANT	115
RETURNS—	
Consolidated	105
Strength	15
Uniform, monthly return of stock	31
SELECTION BOARD—	
Result of, and of Medical Board	107
SICKNESS—	
Insurance and pay during	67
SPECTACLES	66
SPIRITUAL MINISTRATION	47
SUBSTITUTION—	
At home	9
Conditions of	9
Convalescent hospital camps	9
General	8
Motor drivers, overseas	8
Proportionate	8
SURGICAL APPLIANCES	66
TELEGRAMS	13
TRANSFERS—	
Officials	119
Pay on, and authority for fixing	39
TRAVELLING—	
Accommodation, class of	22
Allowance	24
Medical services	62
Authority for movements on duty	22
Cabs, hiring of	23
Claims	25
Expenses on enrolment, etc.	23
Half-fare railway vouchers (Mobile branch only)	25
Hotel charges	26
Meal, standard	26
Motor cars	23
Warrants	22
UNIFORM—	
Accounting	29
Civilian garments, disposal	30

UNIFORM—*continued*.   PAGE.
   Corps colours 30
   Discharged members' 30
   Identity discs 30
   Issue of 26, 125
   Part-worn garments 31
   Returns, monthly, of stocks 31
   Shoes, repair of 29, 126
   Shoulder strap colours 28
   Supply 28
   Useless, rendered useless 31
      Not through members' fault 32
      Overseas 32
      Through members' fault 31

WASHING—
   Board, lodging, service 46
   Household linen 43

WOMEN'S LEGION—
   Motor transport section 48
      Q.M.A.A.C. drivers from overseas fit only home service,
         transfer to 17
      Military cookery section 48